A METHODO...
ON THE ...

BE A DUCK

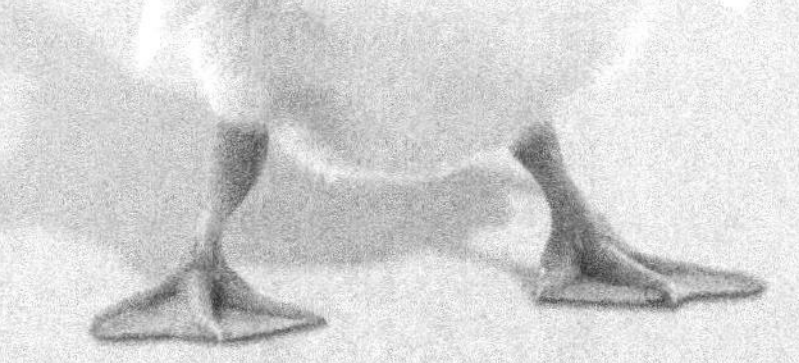

SCOTT JUNIPER

We help busy professionals write and publish their stories
to distinguish themselves and their brands.

(407) 287-5700 | Winter Park, FL
info@BrightRay.com | www.BrightRay.com

ISBN: 978-1-956464-52-8

No part of this publication may be reproduced, stored in a retrieval system, or transmitted in any form or by any means, electronic, mechanical, photocopying, recording, or otherwise, without permission of the author.
For information regarding permission, please contact the author.

Published in the United States of America.
BrightRay Publishing ® 2024

To Jill, Glen, and Faye, AKA Team Juniper

CONTENTS

FOREWORD

Scott Juniper's more than two decades of coaching players at the club, collegiate, and semi-professional levels positions him as a great source of inspiration to lead young people through the transition from youth to adulthood, both on and off the field. His genuine and authentic delivery style is welcomed in the world of youth sports, which is fast becoming more about winning at all costs and making money rather than creating the best environment to develop people and players with skills to last a lifetime.

Juniper's *Be a Duck* is full of wisdom plucked from life experiences while on the path to coaching today's student-athletes. He shares insights on controlling what you can control, working hard/working smart, and owning your independence. Juniper empowers young people to think, ask questions, and decide. His book pokes the reader to reflect on the lessons they learned through influential family members, teammates, and life coaches. It is a lighthearted and empathetic read that sweeps you up in storytelling. You will finish reading *Be a Duck* and then you will want more.

—April Heinrichs, *FIFA High Performance Specialist, FIFA World Cup Winner, and Olympic Gold Medal Coach*

INTRODUCTION

As a kid, I was always busy doing something, but even then, I often looked ahead at what was next. Cub scouts, soccer, swimming, running around the woods, and following the Colchester United Football Club left precious little time for me to stop and *think*. When I did daydream, I'd find myself planning stuff other kids weren't necessarily doing. Imagine 11-year-old me, in my first few weeks of secondary school, cruising into my primary school headmaster's office to let him know that I wanted to help coach the school's soccer team. He graciously listened to my plan and concluded that it was a "nice idea." And that's all it remained: a nice idea. Frustratingly, most of my ideas required permission or help from adults, and I hated to be frozen with inaction.

Around the same time, I was reading the latest Colchester United news in the back pages of the *Evening Gazette* newspaper and spotted an ad that caught my attention: *Colchester half-marathon, sign up here!* I was *in*. When I announced to my dad "I'm going to do this," he was characteristically measured and thoughtful in his response. He smiled, asked if I realised how far that was, and said something about training properly, again calling it a "nice idea." He probably thought my enthusiasm for it wouldn't last long, but I was already snipping the ad from the paper and filling in my details. That year, I ran my first-ever half-marathon.

There were so many excuses I could have used to not follow through. If I'm honest, it was a half-baked idea at best. A far cry from the odd 5k fun run I'd enjoyed with friends. I didn't get close to what I would call proper training, and I don't think Mum and Dad really thought I'd follow through with it until we were at the start line on race day. Not because of a lack of support, but because kids just don't run half-marathons very often. I set a clear goal, made a plan, told people what I was going to do, and I knew I just had to find my wings and take that leap—I had to be a duck.

Decades later, my son wears that 1988 half-marathon shirt to bed. He has even told me he wants to run a half-marathon when he is 10. Younger than I did it. He wants to run it faster than me. I love that. Maybe I can be his "Silver-Caped Superhero" cheering for him at the finish line. Regardless, he and I share a story of what can be achieved when you buckle down, power through excuses, and ignore the conventional guardrails. I still run half-marathons, and I've been coaching soccer for over 30 years. Getting here wasn't easy, and sustaining success at this level demands a daily commitment to excellence. I didn't realise it at the time, but I conceived a vision of a career in coaching at a very young age. That vision shaped my priorities in life, and coaching became my reality. By prioritising life, anyone can transform ideas into reality.

It's the people closest to you who shape your life the most; that's why I often remind my players to prioritise friends who allow them to be the best versions of themselves. Growing up, I had a tight-knit family and a group of great friends who helped shape my values, set my moral compass, and reinforce a mindset that is still part of my framework for coaching today.

Since becoming a parent, I've realised how hard it was for Mum and Dad to manage life for my older brother, younger sister, and me. Total superheroes. Mum worked part-time and coordinated our bonkers schedules. Dad worked harder than anyone I know. His professional discipline lasted a very, very long time, and even though he recently retired, his mindset is the same but focused on fishing, snooker, and sailing.

> *"Bob taught me so much. An inspiring leader, who voiced the importance of staying grounded personality-wise, never fearing failure, and respecting those who you meet all the same."*
>
> —Jonathon Rensink, one of Dad's partners/ colleagues upon his retirement

Whether it's nature or nurture, there are a lot of similarities between my parents and my grandparents. I was lucky enough to have all of my grandparents in my life into adulthood and my great-grandmother for a few years of my childhood. They were the kind of grandparents who had a limitless resource of phrases to keep you honest and coach you through life. You know the ones:

> *Waste not, want not.*
> *Money doesn't grow on trees.*
> *Do as you would be done by.*
> *If at first you don't succeed, try, try, and try again.*

And my all-time favourite:

> *There's no such thing as can't.*

Today's audience may find these mini-lessons too simple to address the nuances of complex modern lives. But consider the context: my grandparents lived as young adults in Britain during the devastating Second World War. Food was rationed, families were torn apart, and their very way of life was at risk on a daily basis.

Grandad Clarke was in the King's Royal Rifle Corps, serving overseas. Grandad Jake worked in a factory making vital parts for the war effort, a "reserved occupation," so he remained in Britain serving with the Home Guard. At the end of the work day, his unit would climb defensive towers and fire rockets at enemy planes as they flew over southeast England. Staring down years of extreme pressure and against all the odds, Britain's Greatest Generation refused to surrender. British stoicism in the face of the horrors of war sent the message that "We are very well, thank you." They would "never yield to the apparently overwhelming might of the enemy," and the national posture was to "keep calm, and carry on."[1,2] Next level resilience.

"An efficient and trustworthy NCO with a quiet and unassuming manner. Honest, reliable, and hardworking."

—Army Form W 3079, Assessment of Military Conduct and Character, Peter W. Clarke (Grandad Clarke)

I was surrounded by loving grandparents with remarkable resilience, but they also knew how to smile and laugh. Regardless of the challenges of the day, they were always "Very well, thank you." Grandma loved baking and wore bold floral dresses and even more floral perfumes. My nan could walk forever, and her house was spotless. The Grandads would sit together at family gatherings and inevitably find something to laugh about. I mean uncontrollable, tears streaming down the face, laughing from the soul. They lived through very tough times, worked extremely hard, had next-level resilience, and made no excuses. They took responsibility and faced their challenges head-on. They knew what was important and showed us how to laugh deeply. Britain's Greatest Generation built a formidable mindset. A mindset that is available to anyone who wants to learn, understand, and apply it as a powerful tool for winning in life.

I've spent a lifetime fascinated by the mindset of human performance. I have vivid memories of the 1984 Olympic Games in Los Angeles watching the likes of Edwin Moses, Daley Thompson, Zola Budd, Carl Lewis, and Steve Ovett. I loved the competitions themselves but was drawn to the stories behind the events. I listened intently to their interviews, waiting for the moment they would reveal what they were thinking as they were competing. I wanted to put their insights into *my* performances. Those Games sparked a lifetime of fascination with the psychology of high performance. I learned very early about the power of positivity and optimism. Later, I studied deliberate mental skills training and the process of weaving it all together in a coaching philosophy. I was a laser-focused single-sport kid early on, but as a teenager, I drew from multi-sport experiences, most notably rugby. My secondary school didn't have a soccer team (until I led the charge to create one in my final year), so I was thrown into rugby. While playing fly-half for the Colchester Royal Grammar School, I learned about a collective warrior spirit and was taught about the New Zealand All-Blacks, and what it meant to sweep the sheds.

I was soccer, soccer, soccer all of the time at that age, so it was an emotional battle to embrace a new sport. Thankfully, it was a brilliant experience. It set me on a path in my career to embrace insights from all sports and blend them into my philosophy of building great teams.

I passed my first coaching licence at age 16. Four years later, I failed the next coaching licence but was able to re-take it the following year and passed. I was embracing inevitable imperfections and building professional humility. By the time I moved halfway around the world to the United States at age 23, I had a lot of coaching experience. I had earned a degree in psychology from the University of Bristol and a master's degree in sport and exercise science from the University of Bath. I had published my research on sport psychology in a peer-reviewed scientific journal and won two national championships as a player, one in high school and another at university. In spite of what I felt was a solid coaching foundation, when I arrived in California, I was just another British accent on the coaching circuit. It was humbling, but I took every opportunity I was offered. I stayed grounded, fought the fear of failure, and committed to doing the very best I could in every role while treating people in the right way along the journey. I was honest, reliable, and hardworking. I put in my time—a lot of time and sacrifice. I committed to this winning mindset, and I never stopped running.

If there's someone who knows about a winning mindset, it's April Heinrichs, who played for and coached the United States women's national soccer team. April captained that team to victory in the 1991 FIFA Women's World Cup in

 BE A DUCK

China and coached the team to a gold medal at the 2004 Olympic Games in Athens. I had read extensively about the USWNT long before I moved to the US. There was one book that stood out about peak performance that compared some of the world's top sports organisations.[3] The authors compared the key elements behind some of the most fearsome teams in world sports, including FC Bayern Munich, the New Zealand All Blacks rugby team, and the United States women's soccer team. There were many references to April's impact in that book, so being invited to interview with her for an assistant coach job was a really big deal for me. Her decision to hire me was one of the most significant inflection points of my career.

I always thought of myself as a hard-working, high-energy, detail-oriented young coach. Then I worked with April, who taught me there was a whole new level. I worked harder with April than any other time I can remember. We were rebuilding the program, which required a sustained commitment to outworking our opponents. We were running for our lives, fuelled by Starbucks chai lattes, and driven by an unapologetically hyper-competitive posture. April taught me to recognize next-level competitors, challenge conventional wisdom and how to see all the moving pieces of an organisation. Maybe the most valuable lessons I learned from her were about friendship. Under April's watch, details were never left unresolved. Every opportunity to grow and innovate was seized. One morning, I arrived at the office and didn't recognise my desk—April walked by and saw my puzzled look. She casually remarked, "Oh yeah, before I left last night I noticed your space was a little disorganised, so I tidied it up for you." You can bet that I keep a neat desk still to this day. April challenged me to be a better coach in so many more ways than a tidy desk. Today, a "tidy desk" is simply a euphemism for striving to be the best professional I can be. April was head-hunted by the US Olympic Committee to join their high-performance team for the Beijing Olympics. Thankfully, I was ready to be a duck and step up to the challenge of being the next head coach at UCI. My time working with April had a profound impact on my personal and professional development, and I'm grateful for the invitation she gave me to learn with her.

You may wonder why I'm willing to share so much of my mindset and methodology with the world. Discourse is the fuel of innovation, and this book is my invitation to you. You can come into our locker room, so to speak, to share some of the biggest lessons I've learned in three decades of coaching. Hopefully, you will feel inspired to embrace transformative ideas and apply them on your own journey to winning in life. Whether you are coaching or playing, lead yourself through these ideas first and you will find yourself impacting those around you. As a head coach, I've refined these ideas through preparation, planning, and execution of hundreds of matches and thousands of hours of practices, presentations, and team meetings. We didn't win all of those matches, but we have won many more than we should have. We have achieved things that have never been done before. We have won championships and been victorious in some of the most remarkable underdog stories in NCAA Division I women's soccer history. There has been no magic wand, just a group of ordinary people with the right priorities and a winning mindset who believed they could achieve extraordinary things. *Why not us?* 🚀

What I am most excited about is we are only just getting started. It's only half-time in my career, and everything in this book is based on what I know *now*. Like half-time in any soccer game, 70 percent of the match is still to come.

The following chapters will lay out the keys to my coaching methodology, but the core of this book is about creating good habits to enhance your life. These lessons are not designed to address clinical matters or chronic illnesses, or to minimize the struggles of mental health—they are for anyone looking to go from good to something special. I want you to maximise your mental game, manage your emotional game, and unlock your spirit for competition. It is my belief that anyone can use these ideas to win in life. To become a better version of yourself. To win the battles. To overcome the hurdles that might seem a long way off or just too big. I will challenge you to radically self-reflect and be brutally honest. To confront your thoughts, reveal your excuses, and wrestle with your self-imposed limits.

You will find yourself becoming a strong and trusted leader. This doesn't need to be the type of leader who sits on a white horse leading an army into battle; begin simply by leading yourself. Make the kinds of small but deliberate and honest changes that compound over time until people respond to your approach to life and follow you. Don't sit on the sidelines and watch your life go by—it's time to smile, step over the "White Line," onto the pitch, and get the very best out of yourself. One step at a time, let's start running.

DOING THE WORK

1. List five influential people in your life.
   a. What lessons did they teach you that are woven into the fabric of who you are?
2. What are your non-negotiables in the way you lead your life or pursue goals?

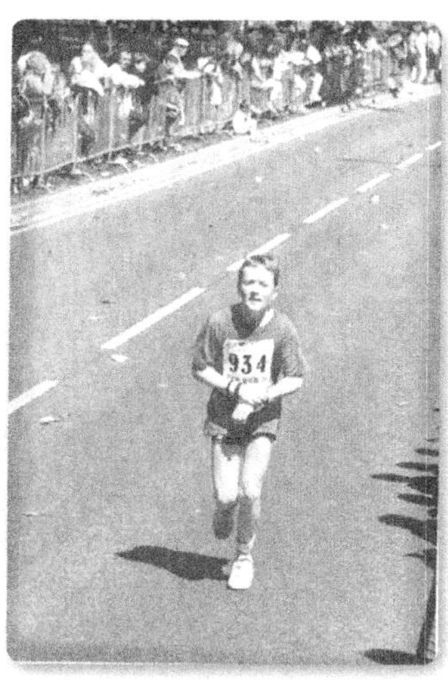

Running that famous first half-marathon at 11 years old.

Nan and Grandad Clarke, my mum's parents, on their wedding day.

Grandma and Grandad Jake, my dad's parents.

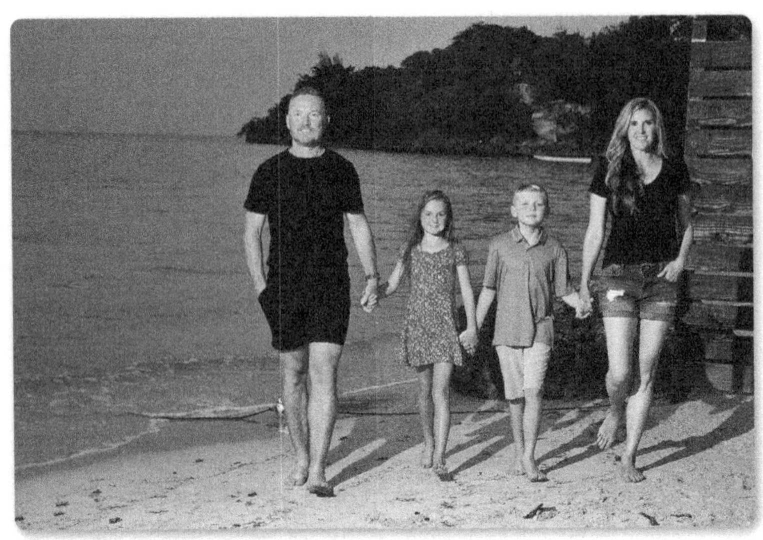

Team Juniper enjoying a vacation to Ocho Rios, Jamaica in June 2024.

Another Team Juniper moment in
November 2023, San Juan Capistrano, CA.

CHAPTER 1
BE A DUCK

A friend of mine is a duck farmer. It seems like one of those random jobs that no one really has, but wouldn't you know, he has one of the largest duck farms in the world. Next-level duck farming. My friend has forgotten more about ducks than the rest of us will ever know put together. One night, while we were at dinner, someone called my friend and said a young duck had somehow made its way into their backyard: "You're a duck guy. What should I do? I don't know how to get this duck out of my yard."

"Don't worry about it," my friend said. "That duck will be a fully grown adult very, very soon. It'll be on its way."

He then explained to me that young ducks have no other way of surviving. They've got a crappy little beak. Floppy, little feet. They're practically useless and highly vulnerable. The only way these defenceless ducklings survive is by growing into adults very quickly.

I love finding engaging ways to explain important concepts, and I knew straight away this was one of those moments. "Be a duck." Grow up. It was perfect—just the ticket as a reminder for my young adults to take responsibility for life, not rely on others to do things for them that they can do for themselves, and stop making excuses.

Working with college athletes, I see young people at a pivotal point in their lives. They don't necessarily have floppy feet and little beaks, but they are learning to be adults, both on and off the field. They are in a transition phase of life as they move from living at home and surviving high school to living on their own and figuring out college life. Shopping, laundry, bills, roommates, and finances are just the start. Many have a tendency to defer those responsibilities back to mom and dad, or to their coaches and academic advisors to fix stuff. Like so many things in life, young people can handle 99 percent of what is thrown at them *if* they are expected to do it for themselves and *if* they are given the time to figure it out. That's why I tell my players—*be a duck.*

They all know what I mean when I say that. It means taking responsibility for the outcomes. Stop blaming other people in your life. Don't blame your teammates. Don't blame the officials. Don't blame your coach!

Be a duck.

The culture of excuses ends when you take responsibility for your outcomes. If you want to be a part of a team and push yourself to become the greatest version of yourself, you need to grow up. Take responsibility for your role on the team and what you have control over. If something goes wrong on the field, be accountable. Off the field, don't be tempted to ask your coach for help doing things that you are more than capable of figuring out for yourself. As a coach, it's hard to resist helping players, especially given that helping others is a driving force in most of us. Of course, there are times when players actually need help or there just isn't the time to learn or figure it out at the moment. Sometimes you just have to choose efficiency. The trick is to know the difference.

If you follow that process, by eliminating unnecessary dependency, you transition from the role of personal assistant to actually being their coach. Then begins the process of coaching yourself out of business by progressively reducing their need for constant instruction. I encourage players to think for themselves, to solve problems in the moment, and embrace the idea of a living and breathing game plan. As a coach, I don't want to develop a co-dependence with my players. I'm just a stepping stone for them. If I do my job properly, they will springboard into the next big phase of their lives, where they'll continue to use their wings.

"I'll ask my mom." "I didn't get a reminder." "Let me check with my dad." "I didn't know I had to do that." I often hear this stuff from our younger players, and I just ask them if it's reasonable to expect them to figure it out themselves—could they just *be a duck*? I'm not asking our players to isolate themselves from their support network, quite the opposite. Once you take responsibility for the things you can do for yourself, your support network is free to help you with new and exciting challenges. As their coach, they don't need me to organise equipment, clean their locker room, remind them to start behind the white line, manage their GPS devices, wash their uniforms, or prompt them to show up for meetings and appointments. They need me to focus on the stuff they can't do. They need me to advocate for them, analyse their performances, scout their opponents, and build their game plans. They need me to teach them *how* to think, not *what* to think. Being a duck isn't easy. I find myself making excuses and deferring responsibility too. The other team won because they have more resources, a bigger support staff, the officials favoured them for one reason or another—they just don't like us! In reality, it's all just a cop-out. There might be a kernel of truth in some of these things, but leaning on tired old excuses blinds you from seeing precious opportunities to improve.

Acknowledge the excuses that fight their way into your thoughts. Take a moment to honestly reflect on what you're making excuses for and redirect yourself toward accountability for your outcomes. Over time, make a list, write them down, and hold yourself accountable. Coach yourself like you would coach your own players; support yourself like you would support a friend; guide yourself like you would guide your little brother or sister. By actively bringing excuses to the forefront of your consciousness and honestly labelling them, you can redirect the excuse-building machine into an ownership, accountability, and responsibility process of high-performance growth. A far more powerful and satisfying posture.

You have more control over your life than you realise, and if you deliberately spend time identifying excuse-making in yourself, you'll be better able to see it in others in your orbit. You will notice that the players on your team or the people in your organisation fit into two basic categories: There are those who lean into excuses as a way to do less, avoid hard work, or hide from accountability. The others reject excuses, demand accountability for themselves and others, and lean into the hard work and bigger challenges. I'll leave it to you to figure out who the winners are. Guide yourself and others to reject excuses and take ownership of their outcomes—grow and repeat.

No matter how old you are, you never stop growing. Your frame of reference will shift. I have to remind myself to "Be a duck" with regular frequency. Inevitably, as you move through life, you take on new responsibilities simply because you have to. You are never 100 percent ready for marriage, a mortgage, or kids, but we manage to figure it out given time. The key is to recognize the excuses that linger because we aren't forced by our natural circumstances to confront them. Challenge yourself to honestly reflect on how to take responsibility for them. How long do you really need to live at home with your parents after you graduate? Are you prioritising lifestyle over responsibility? Maybe the new car, phone, clothes, shoes, eating out, concerts, and vacations aren't all that essential until you can pay the rent. Every once in a while, I still find myself on the phone with my mom, and I catch myself venting about one challenge or another. If my tone slides toward an excuse, Mum will redirect me pretty fast. "I just don't have time" gets the classic response: "You have the same amount of time as everyone else," and we're back on track. Vent with supportive people who will listen, absorb, reflect with you, and redirect you back toward being a duck.

The human condition guarantees you will experience excuses forming regularly in your consciousness. Far from being a problem, be thankful you have something to fight, something to push back against, and many opportunities to win. If we didn't have anything to push back against, we'd slither through life with relative ease but minimal growth. Acknowledging when a thought is an excuse is the first step to beating it. Honest self-reflection is a powerful tool, and confronting the excuse with a solution, a plan, and a positive response are steps in the process toward taking responsibility for your life, owning your outcomes, good and bad, and ultimately winning in life.

In our locker room, I sometimes see the excuse ecosystem in full effect. When a player realises they are not in the starting line-up, sometimes that player decides to host a pity party. The emotional response in their excuse ecosystem is now fully awake. The mind is offering up thoughts such as "That's not fair," or "That's just favouritism." The excuses are manifested outwardly as negative body language and mad-dog eyes intended to invite others to join their party. The blame game is unfolding in their mind, and some of their fellow ducklings feel drawn to attend the party to console and reinforce those feelings. The adult ducks on the team will not attend the party. Some just march out of the locker room, their minds focused fully on the game, but one or two might absorb a brief vent from their young teammate before quickly redirecting to honest self-reflection. Very quickly, the ducks are marching, with their shoulders back, out of the locker room, down the tunnel to the stadium, and the ducklings have no choice but to hurry along behind them. When no one is left at the pity party, it's over.

We work hard to give our players a clear understanding about playing time decisions, and we encourage dialogue as a part of the process. Honest self-reflection and feedback are important. The more we identify excuses and build a culture of responsibility, the more effective we are—the faster we grow. Responsibility extends to every aspect of our team. They learn from the New Zealand All Black tradition to clean up after themselves in the locker room, to "sweep the shed." They organise the equipment for practice and games, they manage their team kit, and they are accountable for loading it onto the bus for trips. They participate in grocery store runs on the road, finding restaurants, checking in for hotels and flights, and they have a plan to meet their personal nutrition needs. We have excellent staff, but we don't have a bloated team of equipment managers, directors of operations, nutritionists, and travel agents to handle life for our players. I think we grow up faster as a result. Better ingredients for winning. We are not focused on what we can do to make life easier or more comfortable. Our staff focuses on things the players can't do for themselves, the things that make our race car a little faster.

As a dad, I try to have the same philosophy at home. At seven and nine years of age, my kids can dress themselves, make their breakfast, brush their teeth, do their hair, tie their laces, and pack their bags. They are also learning how to wash a car and use a leaf blower. Just like all parents, we jump in and speed those things up when we are running late, but when we have the time to let them figure it out, they can do most of it themselves with supervision! My daughter's french toast on a Sunday morning is not exactly how I would do it, but it tastes delicious. The pink and black sweatpants aren't my wife's favourite combo for her to wear to school, but she loves to express herself. My son's choice to wear a Liverpool jersey to school is his own, certainly not mine, and he can only deal with the smaller trash cans on trash day, for now.

His hair is sometimes up, sometimes down, or swept to the side, and occasionally what he calls "fluffy." He's making his own choices. When they are taking care of the little things for themselves, we can do other things for them.

My kids, like my players, will eventually face life in the real world. When they do jump into the real world and they have to take on naturally occurring responsibilities, I hope they can fly. I know they're watching me as a role model. All I can do is tackle my responsibilities head-on, without excuses, and hope they learn from my example. After all, that's what it means to be a duck.

DOING THE WORK

1. List three things you could do for yourself that you let others do for you.
2. Think of a time you have blamed someone, other than yourself, for something you could assume responsibility for moving forward.
3. Which excuses do you want to eliminate from your approach to life?

CHAPTER 2

. . . AND HAVE FUN!

For several years, I was a season ticket holder for the Colchester United soccer team. I was completely absorbed. A young die-hard fan. We had relegation and promotion. Heartbreak and glory. My Uncle Pete would take me to the home games. I'd travel for hours on buses for the away games. It was often so cold when we would line up for a cuppa tea at half-time. Uncle Pete would buy me chips, the preferred diet of any boy. I always drenched them in cheap tomato ketchup and ate them while wearing my woollen gloves. The smell of the sauce would linger on those gloves for weeks. The weather would be miserable, and yet, it was the epitome of fun.

As a young lad, I was the kid always looking for more fun during a school lesson. I wasn't the class clown, but I was one of the first to join the joke. At the all-boys school I attended, you were either learning French or learning how to mess with the French teacher. And I was often in the latter crowd.

There was a time when a group of us planned to show up late for French class. We walked in, one by one, and made the apology, "Je suis désolé, madame pour je suis arrivé en retard." We thought our pronunciation was impeccable. "Asseyez vous," she would say with a smile. Messing with professors was our profession in school, but I felt very differently when playing soccer.

There's time to play and time to be serious. For me, French class was very different from sports. That sort of fun didn't translate to the soccer field. I was focused in a different way when I was lacing up the boots and heading out to the pitch at kick-off. It didn't matter if it was a cup final or recess! I didn't like it when others didn't view soccer as I did. Looking back, I'm sure some of my classmates didn't appreciate my approach to French class either. Or for that matter, Latin, music, and physics.

"Do your best … and have fun" were often the last words I heard from my mum as I ran out of the car to play a soccer match. I found comfort in those words. Both things were well within my control, and as a kid, I had the most fun when I was immersed in playing. I wanted to outwork, outthink, and outscore everyone, all with a smile on my face. It took me a long time to understand the differences between cheeky "school" fun and fully immersed "sports" fun. The English language doesn't easily support that distinction, or perhaps I just haven't built the lexicon yet. As best as I can explain it, one thing is a wonderfully light-hearted, "banterous" fun, while the other is a soulful, fully immersed sense of joy.

We call them both fun, but they are very different. Both amazingly important, but the wisdom in high performance is knowing the difference and guiding your team toward the right one at the right time. Giving my best effort was enough to make my mum and dad proud. It still is.

As sports become more competitive, as kids get older, as sports parents become more invested, the fun elements can quickly get pushed aside. On one occasion, I heard a coach yell at his team, "Do you think this is just a game?!" When the goal is to win at all costs, it's not difficult to understand how the fun of sports is lost. At nearly all levels of sports now, coaches lose their jobs if they don't win enough. Under the pressure to win immediately, how do you balance the need for fun and winning at the same time?

What I often see is the *fun-work-fun* solution. These teams have a lot of fun before the game and sometimes during warm up, take a break from fun for just long enough to get through a game, and then get back to the fun, after holding their breath for the post-game tirade. The game is stressful for these teams. They play in a mechanical way, without the freedom to express themselves; they don't take risks; they lack bravery to confront the hardest parts of the game; they play scared. The exhilaration of scoring goals is replaced by relief. Ultimately, players begin to burnout and the love for the game is lost. These coaches squeeze the talent out of the players who are ultimately replaced. A fatally transactional proposition for the player.

I've chosen to challenge the fallacy that fun and hard work are on opposite ends of a spectrum. In other words, I want to bend that conventional spectrum until the ends of it are touching, overlapping, unified. You have to have fun to work hard, and in competitive sports, you have to work hard to have fun. Define "fun" as a deep feeling of joy only experienced when you are fully immersed in what you are doing each day. That should be the feeling you have when you step over the White Line. Train to think in the "Now and Next," in the present and near future. Move on from errors, reward bravery, and don't weigh yourself down with the burdens of outcomes beyond the immediate next moment. The outcomes will take care of themselves if you stay in the now. As Grandma liked to say, "Take care of your pennies and the pounds will take care of themselves." Reduce your time frame of focus to something as small as possible. The now. The present. Play there because it's where joy lives, and it's a space in time that anxieties can't go, as hard as they try. Do your best *and have fun.*

You can apply the same principle of being fully present off the field too. Part of our team culture is being phone-free during team meals, in the training room, during team-walks, and from a designated time before kick off on game days. A game that takes us on the road for three to five days at a time, in and out of hotels—that's a lot of shared meals and traditional game-day meditation walks together. The players leave their phones in their rooms. Not silenced in their pockets—*in their rooms.* From the moment they leave their rooms, they interact differently. They have to. These times give us space for teammates to engage with one another, more fully immersed. It's taken me years to find the right balance. After a few years of taking myself too seriously, I began writing " . . . and have fun" in the bottom corner of the whiteboard in our locker room. Those words have got bigger and bigger and rank higher and higher in the game plan. It's not too late to have more fun—it's time for you to bring the fun to the top of your list.

When I moved to the United States, I hardly knew anything about John Wooden. Someone very early on told me, "If you're going to coach in the United States, you have to know all about John Wooden." So I read a lot of books. I read extensively about coaches like Phil Jackson, Pat Summit, Pat Riley, Vince Lombardi, and, of course, John Wooden. I fell in love with his Pyramid of Success. Years later, I met Tim and Peanut Harper from the nonprofit, Harper For Kids. Peanut Harper, a top 20 player on the WTA tour during her pro tennis career, had worked with John Wooden to write a children's book, *Inch and Miles: The Journey to Success*, which explains his Pyramid of Success to kids. I join Harper for Kids to visit elementary schools and talk about character development and leadership. Tim always puts me on the spot in front of hundreds of kids with questions. "Scott, what is your definition of success?"

I fumbled my way through the answer to that one a few times and later took the time to really reflect on it. I knew I had to commit to something that authentically represented what I'm about: **success is finding joy in the pursuit of your biggest, boldest dreams**.

There are different types of joy in life. Joy can be as simple and perfect as laughing with friends. It can be travelling to explore new places, new adventures, new hobbies.

For me, the greatest joy is being utterly and completely immersed in an activity I'm passionate about. It's crystalized in my definition of success. This means being truly present in the moment. Not in a "Live, Laugh, Love" kind of way but rather tapping into a flow state, channelling every last ounce of your energy into the task at hand. Kids do it instinctively. When they are playing, whether it be with blocks, action figures, or dolls, kids are in the fun flow state. They aren't worried about the past or future. They play in that joyful moment. It's our natural state. As we get older, we lose this inherent ability for play; culture and society beat it out of us and expect us to keep things serious. It sets up a work versus fun paradigm. As coaches, it's part of our job to move our players back into their natural state, aligned with joy. We are more likely to perform well there, to win more on the pitch, and win more in life.

This lesson was crystalized for me in 2021 coaching a precocious talent from San Diego. She was an incredible athlete and soccer player with a hunger for winning and a low level of tolerance for anyone who didn't want to win with her. She was spicy. I love that in players. Until it gets too hot that is. On one occasion her spiciness was very hot, debilitatingly hot. She was mad, angry even. We subbed her out of the game, and she was predictably mad about that and everything else. In the next few days, we found time to talk, and I learned that she had a lot of family at the game. It was in San Diego, and I hadn't really considered that the location would shift some variables. She wanted so badly to win, to play well for her family and score goals, that it had become overwhelming. Through those conversations I learned a lot about her mindset. We made changes over time to her role on our team, and I adjusted the way we would coach her. We shifted the emphasis of her role from attacking a specific space or opponent to giving her the freedom to explore the pitch and attack the players and spaces she saw. We talked a lot about how to have fun and play with a smile without compromising the competitive edge. I probably coached her less and less in the traditional sense as the season went on. It's a reminder that sometimes you simply have to remove the barriers. Scarlett Camberos was always very good, but she was unbeatable in the second half of that season. The balance of trust, freedom, winning, and fun gave her the room to express herself in her most natural state. Scarlett could have played one more year at UCI but chose to make the brave decision to turn pro. It was the right decision. She has crushed it in the pros, and she's only getting started.

A snapshot of me smiling before the UCI vs UCLA first-round NCAA game in November of 2021. *Photo Credit: Sandra Velez-Lopez*

Does It Look Like I'm Having Fun?

There's the picture of me smiling on the sidelines at our big game against UCLA in 2021. You would think it was after the game, after we had won, but it was actually before the game even started. It's taken many years to begin understanding it, but these days I try not to take myself too seriously. I sometimes wear bright shoes and bright pink socks on game days as a reminder to have fun *and* focus, without sacrificing one for the other.

I'll have a laugh and smile during a game, but every fibre of my being will be fully immersed in what we're doing. If you ever play laser tag with me, I'll be a silent ninja assassin the moment the game starts. If you wanna try go-karts, I'll be Formula One as soon as the light turns green.

When I was hired as the head coach at UC Irvine, I was only 29 years old—really young in my world. I naturally felt like I needed to compensate to be taken seriously. It took me grit and grind to reach this level in my career so early, and I purposely dialled back my personality. I can admit now that I overcompensated; I thought I had to be super serious to have people take me seriously. As the pressure mounts in the thick of coaching a big game, it's easy to lose yourself and suck the fun out of everything. As the coach, your emotions influence the emotions of the whole team. All it takes is a slight shift in the tone of your voice and a couple of adverse comments to lose the mojo between you and the team. The stakes are high; if you're not mindful, you can quickly fall into a negative vortex and lose the connection for the rest of the game.

Coaching has natural highs and lows. It's just a part of the deal. If I found myself in a funk back then, or if I noticed that I was taking myself too seriously (filled with negative emotions about the team, the job, the previous game), I'd call my mate, Rich. He always had a camp or clinic he wanted me to do or a player I should look at, so there was always an easy excuse to ring him. Most of the time, I just wanted a laugh. He was a fellow British coach who had been in the US a lot longer than me. Without even knowing it, he always found a way to get me back where I needed to be. He was a performer, a singer, a dancer, a storyteller, and a great coach. His players loved him. They still do. During games, Rich would ask the officials to make a substitution and then try to substitute the referees—a classic Rich move. The world lost Richard Boon way too early. I miss him, but he still makes me smile.

Summer of Fun

In 2018, I was asked to build a semi-professional women's team for a soccer club in Southern California. It was only for a three-month summer season, but I was excited for the opportunity to go full throttle to test the idea of maximising fun *and* winning at the same time.

I wanted to ensure these players had the most fun they could ever have playing on a summer league team. When I told the club this was going to be the core focus, they were a little taken aback at first. They were hiring me because of my experience, and they assumed that my resume would be enough to draw good players. I told them to trust me. I knew that when I told prospective players, "This is going to be the most fun you have ever had playing soccer, and we're going to win," I'd be able to build an incredible team.

The LA Galaxy Orange County Women became the single best semi-professional women's soccer team that's ever existed (I stand by that!). We even won the National Championship the following year. We blended former pro players with long and successful careers like Olympic gold medalist, Natasha Kai, and four-time All-American, Lindsey Huie, with future US Women's National Team players like Catarina Macario, Taylor Kornieck, and Jenna Nighswonger (who had barely finished high school). We had a clear identity; the players had the freedom to express themselves; there were no egos; we were brave; we won and had a great time doing it.

When they are running out of the car, I tell my kids to do their best . . . and have fun. I tell them that I can't wait to watch them play. In my pre-game team talks, I tell my players the same things. They lean into it and can't wait for what's next, and the energy keeps growing. As the coach, I have to be the model for the team and show them how to be competitive but also love, love, love what we're doing. We all have to be 100 percent immersed without reservations or hesitations. If we get it wrong, we're gonna get it wrong—but we're gonna get it wrong while being fully immersed in what we've set out to do.

1. List the five most fun things you have done this week.
   a. What makes them fun?
2. Who are the people you enjoy spending time with the most?
   a. What makes them so fun to be around?
3. Think of a time you were so fully immersed in an activity you forgot about time.

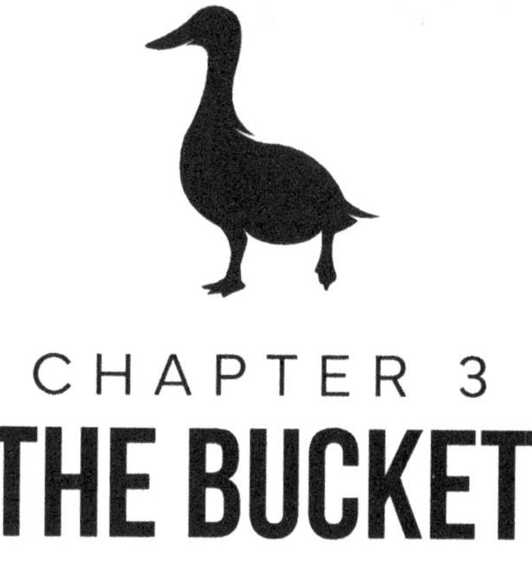

CHAPTER 3
THE BUCKET

"Sounds like there's a hole in your bucket," my grandparents would say any time I started up with excuses. An excuse wasn't a reason to abandon the cause. My family was always kind but firm; an excuse was redirected into an invitation to find a solution. Think of the childhood song: "There's a hole in my bucket, dear Liza, dear Liza." It's the same sort of principle; there's a constant stream of excuses from Henry on one side, with Liza inviting Henry to consider solutions on the other. A hole is a major problem if you're a bucket . . . unless you fix it. You use straw to fill the hole—the straw needs to be cut? Then cut the straw with the axe; the axe is dull? Then sharpen it. The song, to me, is a nice reflection of the inevitable internal dialogue we all experience.

Be a duck is, in some senses, the first step here. You have to take responsibility for the outcome before you can fully confront the hole in your bucket. We have a tendency to fall into the quicksand of the excuse-making ecosystem when things get a little tough. It's easy to hop on the excuse train and bail on the task at hand. And it's certainly more comfortable.

So why put in the work? Because an axe doesn't get sharper without friction. You can't grow and elevate without doing the work. It's a natural part of the human condition to make excuses; having them doesn't make you lazy or unmotivated. It's what you do with them that defines you.

I use a pretty basic mental framework: it's basically a text message thread. A conversation with the inevitable excuses. When they arrive, I just fire back a quick response. My best available solution. If another excuse pops up in the line below, a fresh response is required. Just repeat until the excuses are exhausted, but beware of the shifting excuse. As you begin to win the battle, your excuses will morph from their original form, shifting the discussion to what they hope is a new weak point. "Yeah, but . . ." will preface the new excuse, and in that moment, you know you are winning. The excuse ecosystem is running out of fuel. It may gather up all of its remaining energy for one last push, a bit like when you're trying to put the kids to bed at night. They get a bit crazy, but that's the moment to stay strong; you are about to win. Your unwavering innovation, creativity, positivity, and optimism have more energy than excuses have in all their forms, so choose to keep going until your solutions win. The text bubbles will suggest one last effort is brewing, but the message won't appear. A win.

As a dad of two high-energy ducklings and with a job that eviscerates time, I have a steady stream of excuses for not getting things done. It's easy to say that I have no time. No time to run, for instance. In fact, I tried that excuse a long time ago, but my assistant coach at the time, Kendall Fletcher, provided the accountability that day: "How much time do you need? Are you really saying you can't make 20 minutes in your day?"

Well, it's really hot outside—nobody wants to do a workout if you're already sweating just lacing up your shoes.

So I invested in a treadmill. Regardless of the tempestuous Newport Beach climate, I had eliminated the weather excuse. But . . . there was another excuse waiting behind that one:

It's boring to run on a treadmill.

I could have let that be my downfall: spaced out my runs or cut them short because it's too boring running in the garage. But I wouldn't let myself do that; I installed a TV, and I put something on—often soccer, sometimes Prison Break. Just enough of a distraction to drown out the excuses. I have run a lot of treadmill miles watching Michael Schofield escape and get re-captured and escape again.

But . . . it gets hot in the garage.

So I installed a huge fan.

Yeah, but if I workout, I'll have to shower, change, and wash my hair—that's a lot of time.

So I gave myself a buzz cut.

Yeah but . . . I can do it later.

So I put a big sign on the wall: *NOW*. This was a particularly powerful level of accountability since I've used that word as a rallying cry for my team over the years. I never ask my players to do something I wouldn't or haven't done myself.

Then, I run. I'm not about to let excuses rule me, but you have to make that choice for yourself and decide that ideas and solutions will win the day.

Among many other achievements in her life, Kendall was part of the University of North Carolina team, which won

27 straight games on their way to a National Championship in 2003. She was my Silver-Caped Superhero that day and gave me a lifetime response for that particular excuse. A gift that keeps on giving.

"I've always taken on multiple challenges at the same time. When I was coaching at UCI, I was also still playing pro. On a big recruiting day, we would show up early in the morning and be at the field all day. I would just go to bed early, get up at 3 a.m., and get my workout in. If you really want something, you will find the time to get it done."

—Kendall Fletcher (UCI 2007–2009,
NCAA National Champion, Pro Player, Coach)

Managing time has become my single most effective tool for beating excuses. Our team has a framework of priorities that helps everyone make the important decisions on how to organise the demands of a high-performance life. Prioritise your *health and well-being* as your number one. If you are healthy and strong, you can take care of your *family* obligations and responsibilities. After that, our players focus on anything directly related to their career. Only then do we ask them to focus on *soccer*. The final category is *everything else*. The normal stuff: the beach, the movies, travel, snowboarding trips, music festivals, birthday celebrations, etc. If you take care of your priorities in the right order, you can win in every facet of your life and have plenty of bandwidth to enjoy *everything else*.

My schedule isn't entirely my own, what with kids and an entire team to manage. As Bruce Lee taught us, "Be water, my friend." In his famous inspirational speech about water, he said, "You put it in a teapot, it becomes the teapot." So when I'm driving the kids to ninja class, I become a ninja! I need to flow with the schedule and move where I'm needed to address life's demands. I flow with the family schedule, my team's practices, and in the free spaces, I can focus on growth in whichever lane has the most juice. It's about learning to live in the healthy extremes rather than searching for perfect balance each day.

As a student-athlete, the championship season and final exams sometimes collide, but you can learn to live in that healthy extreme for long enough to win. Be water, my friend. Beyond the extremes, you can define your sacred time, carefully placing the teapot around which your world can flow. Eight o'clock is storytime with my kids. For the team, sacred time is game day. After breakfast, we meet in the hotel lobby and head out on our grounding Meditation Walk. It's 20 minutes of time, no phones, listening to the world, enjoying the now, and strengthening our mindset in preparation for the game. We put away the distractions on game day—they'll still be around tomorrow and will otherwise become the perfect source of excuses if you "drop the ball."

Over time, you will win. It might not be a perfectly straight line; there will be better days than others. Running has become one of my chosen laboratories for decoding the human condition, managing doubt, and building a winning mindset, but it's a constant process. The half-marathon is my sweet spot. Long enough to be a serious challenge but manageable enough to fit in the training around my crazy schedule. When I was running my last half-marathon, I found myself grappling with an entire ecosystem of excuses.

I had already done most of the work: the training, roads, hills, and the treadmill. It is also the planning, logistics, recovery, and getting my toe on the line at sunrise for the start of the race. If you prepare well, it can be a lot of fun for the first few miles. Legs feel fresh and springy, and you find yourself among a group of similarly bouncy runners. It's in the last few miles that things change. The legs get really heavy, the feet are sore, and you can start feeling sorry for yourself. My excuse ecosystem kicked into overdrive. Other runners around me looked fresher, bouncier, and seemed to be having more fun than me.

"Their running shoes are better than mine."

"I don't have the time they have to train."

"I missed the last water station."

"They have a whole running club to do this with."

"That runner is much younger than me, no wonder they are going faster."

"That runner is way older and more experienced than me, no wonder they are going faster than me!"

My point here is simple. The goal isn't to eliminate the negative thoughts and excuses—they are inevitable. The goal is to recognize them for what they are and counter them with solutions. Again and again and again. I've learned to do that, and it actually puts a smile on my face as I'm heading for the finish line. The game comes alive in a different way in the last two miles with a new opponent. *Me.* It took me quite a few attempts to run the 13.1 miles in under 1 hour, 40 minutes. My PR is 1 hour, 33 minutes. My goal in my 40s is to run every year in one hour, plus my age in minutes. I ran a solid 1:45 this year. Two minutes to spare. A win.

If you don't dismantle your ecosystem of excuses, you stop pushing and you stop growing. Some people are okay with that, but if you're still reading this book, you're most likely a high achiever. Or you at least want to be. You're hungry for the challenge and willing to work. That said, there's a difference between lying down and resting. The first is when you give up because the work is too hard. The latter is when you take a break because the ascent is exhausting. So ask yourself, am I resting before the next stage of the climb or am I lying down in defeat hiding behind excuses? Some players have constant ascension for the four years they spend with me; others hit plateaus in between solving problems, fixing their blindspots, and mastering skills. As a coach, it's my responsibility to juggle these nuances and create intentional plateaus for individuals and the team as a whole to rest, reflect, and regenerate. Sometimes, pausing to take a look back over your shoulder at what you've achieved and reflecting on that for a while is just the fuel you need to attack the next challenge. It's up to the players to test their limits, honestly reflect for a moment, and determine if they're just regenerating and preparing to attack the next one or heading back down the mountain on the excuse train.

For myself, I try to remain relentless in that growth mentality. *Now* is always the time for action. Sometimes you have to learn something new, find a different pathway, or innovate to solve a problem. Sometimes I'm physically exhausted, creatively spent, mentally drained, and emotionally done, but I'm rarely empty on all levels at the same time. I've learned that you can always move forward if you just choose the right lane. Beat excuses. I've incorporated that mindset into the fabric of our team. In the arms race of college athletics, we are David versus Golliath in so many ways, but we never allow a challenge to limit growth. Problems are just barriers we have to overcome and opportunities we are grateful to have been given. In fact, we deliberately seek out the biggest challenges. We put those challenges in front of the team and see what happens, like when we take on tough opponents in hostile environments. We may not win them all, but Texas A&M University in the heat of College Station and BYU at altitude in Provo are not games for the weak. We found a way to win in both those places. We have regularly overcome big deficits in resources. Victories over Arizona, Arizona State, Auburn, Cal, Oregon, Oregon State, UCLA, USC, and Wake Forest are perfect examples. We respect our opponents in only the right ways. We have to develop a high clarity game plan and galvanise a shared emotional buy-in to that plan. Our living game plan must be bold, brave, and broad enough to absorb the unknowns and chaos of competition. We might be David, but we will be "very well, thank you," and we will "never, ever, ever give in."

DOING THE WORK

1. What are your worst daily excuses for not getting stuff done?
    a. List solutions for each one.

CHAPTER 4

THE MONSTER IN YOUR POCKET

Self-talk is a concept that spans centuries, cultures, and thousands of miles. Even Plato had a piece of wisdom to share on it: "The soul when thinking appears to me to be just talking—asking questions of herself and answering them, affirming and denying."[4] Pretty transformative stuff . . . but a little bit boring right?

Let me introduce the monster in your pocket. That's the little voice of your thoughts, the internal dialogue that chimes in whenever you face down a challenge or task. It's not inherently positive or negative. It's simply your emotions dancing with cognition and performance. If you work through this concept your monster's voice will become quite distinct, familiar, and unique to you; it's always emotional in one way or another—happy and energetic but also scared and defeatist at times. The first step in the way I conceptualise the life of my little monster is to move him out of my head and into my pocket. He's only small, so he is quite comfortable. I can still hear him, but he can't dictate the way I operate from there. In fact, in my best moments, I'm fully in charge of my monster; he's completely locked down. He's never completely going away so the best I can do is make friends and get to know him.

Remember: not all monsters are inherently bad, scary, or evil—think *Monsters, Inc.* and *Where the Wild Things Are*; these can show you the range of what a monster can be. Start to recognize when the monster is awake, rearing its little head from your pocket. When you hear your monster trying to influence the way you perform, give it a name, a face, a haircut maybe. Add colour, a style, and personality traits until you have a vivid concept of who your monster is. Make them a little friend of yours; my monster is named Hendrick. Hendrick is bright red like Animal from the Muppets, and he loves wearing different hats to match his mood. He has a baseball hat, a cowboy hat, a top hat, and a flying helmet with goggles. He fits in the palm of my hand. I can even squeeze him in my fist for a while, and he will pop back into full form when I let go.

If I'm on a run, Hendrick is always reminding me how long the run is. Most days, he even questions why we're even bothering to run in the first place. In the final stretch of a run he gets pretty loud and tries to take control of that dance between my emotions, cognition, and performance so I have conceptualised a mini-drone for him. I send him off on missions to keep him busy while I stay locked in. I'll send him in his drone to chase the bird with a fish in its mouth or check out the other side of the bay to find an egret or a heron. Just to get rid of him for 5 or 10 minutes. I'm in control. I'll need him with me at the finish line for some positive self-talk though—*Scott! Nice running. Your time even improved. You look great. Good work.* That dialogue becomes a source of great joy and celebration.

The key is to move your monster from a position of control to a position of support and learn to manage your interactions. For me, Hendrick is a wild looking monster. For you, it could be an exotic bird sitting on your shoulder, a fluffy cloud, or just a blob! It doesn't matter. The important part is that you can conceive of a separation between your emotions, cognition, and performance.

That internal dialogue you have is completely natural. Recent studies show that children first engage in self-talk around the same time they start speaking in sentences, around two or three. That self-talk slowly internalises as children get older and develops into inner speech.[5] Self-talk is a constant flow of positive and negative thoughts. The thoughts themselves are not a problem; it's what you do with the dialogue that will chart the course of your life.

You may know the parable of the two wolves. They are both inside us, and they are always fighting. One is good; one is evil—or rather, one is positive; one is negative. And the one that wins the battle is the one you feed. In this story, notice that the wolves are separate and distinct from their host, and it is the host who can assume complete control if they are active and deliberate with their interactions. The human condition requires us to be active in this process in order to succeed. Passivity leads down a very different path.

Controlling self-talk gets harder as emotions grow stronger or when we are physically depleted. This could be in the critical moments of a match, maybe in the final five minutes. Perhaps it is in the last mile of a run or the final repetitions of a tough workout. Regardless, you can push yourself to speak positively, but despite your best efforts, the negative wolf will have plenty to eat at times. The monster in your pocket is both wolves; it will have positive and negative things to say. The goal is not to eliminate those emotions. That's fruitless; they are inevitable. But when nerves, self-doubt, and anxiety hit—or that ugly stress—you are best placed to manage your internal environment and your performance if you have taken the time to get to know your monster really well. You will know how to recognize the warning signs of its growing influence, how to separate from it, and have a strategy to keep it quiet while you perform.

I see it in myself, and I constantly see it in athletes: self-doubt. *You can't do that. You'll look stupid. People are going to laugh. You're not good enough. Don't speak up. Stay quiet. Pause. Wait.* It's important to remember that self-doubt can come in so many forms. It isn't always obvious. Even those who appear the most confident still carry their share of self-doubt. Tanya Taylor became an All-American at UCI in 2010 and was drafted by the Boston Breakers. If you had the pleasure of watching her play, you would have seen an incredibly brave and courageous player who frightened her opponents every time she got the ball. In reality, while Tanya was genuinely a confident individual in a lot of aspects of her life, self-doubt still crept in. We would talk before most games to remind her of what she was capable of, and even after an All-American season, she had doubts about her ability to play at the next level. Of course, Tanya rose above those doubts, completing a successful soccer career by being inducted into the UCI Athletics Hall of Fame, and she now runs her own law firm.

—Tanya Taylor, Esq. (UCI 2007–2011, UCI Athletics Hall of Fame)

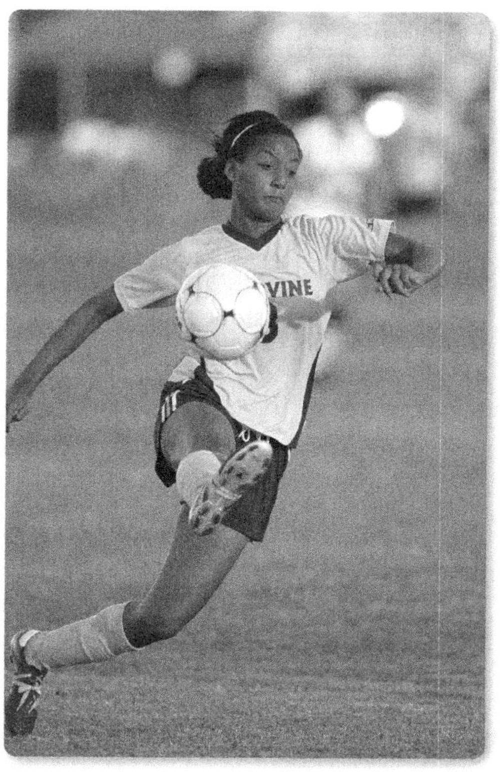

Tanya Taylor in action as she helped secure our victory over Wake Forest in the second round NCAA game in November 2010.

Our emotions play an important role in guiding us safely through life, and for that reason, they need to be the fastest messages to arrive in our internal discussion. To perform well in sports, we need to stare down these emotions and bc brave. Nod to these first emotional thoughts; acknowledge them. These are from the little monster in your pocket. Arriving immediately behind the emotional first thoughts are your second thoughts. Less reactive, more responsive, more cognitive, and more effective for decision-making in performance. If you can learn the difference between first and second thoughts, you will feel the difference in your performances. It doesn't always have to be a big-scale, high-stress event like a competition or a soccer game; it can be as simple as your monster wanting you to keep watching the latest Netflix series. Now your future self will appreciate you going to bed at a reasonable time, but that monster in your pocket may whisper, "Just one more episode." Rather than submit to your monster's wishes, make your future self the priority.

The monster may start in your pocket, but it doesn't have to live there forever. Give it a drone. Give it wings. Give it a little car to drive around. Let it run free, away from your ears. Be careful though: do not ever let your monster talk to someone else's monster. My wife and I understand that we both have this reactive emotional side. Our little monsters are even louder if we disagree. If Hendrick speaks directly to Matilda, we are headed for trouble. They are both reactive, first thoughts hammering other first thoughts. The key to maintaining positive communication is not letting our monsters speak to each other. Allow the second thoughts, the ones with more considered content, to lead. This goes for talking to other players, coaches, teachers—whomever it may be. Your rational self is always going to be the better communicator. Wait for the second thought—you don't have to wait long.

Remember, you are the dominant force in the relationship between you and your monster. When I talk to Hendrick, I make it a very direct internal dialogue. I ensure Hendrick is quiet when he needs to be quiet and that he and I interact at the right time and in the right place. Unfortunately, sometimes I don't do a good job of monitoring our relationship, and he can sneak up on me. This is usually during very tense games. He can jump in and drag me into a brief conflict with a referee, an opposing coach, or whoever happens to be in close proximity. The monster isn't there to blame. You can make it serve you; it's a tool to parse out your emotions. You get to control how you respond. Remember: be a duck.

Hendrick getting the better of me as I argue with the ref (it's been no hard feelings—I often have this ref at our games).

As a player, you should know that self-doubt is not in and of itself a bad thing. Sometimes that self-doubt comes up during conditioning for our team. Players have to ask themselves: is the monster holding me back, or am I actually too exhausted to continue? By engaging in dialogue, you can recognize the difference.

It's your job to dominate that self-doubt—a monster in your pocket just happens to be a useful way of conceptualising your emotions to keep them separate and distinct from yourself. As a coach, it is my job to teach players that the emotional side of the human condition is distinct from the rational. All I can do is introduce them to their monster and coach them on their ability to dominate that internal conversation—it's up to them to do the rest.

Your monster may dominate here and there, but as long as you're in dialogue with it, you'll have more constructive self-talk. The monster in your pocket is a part of you, so accept it. Make it silly. Make it weird. And laugh at it. Your monster may say some negative things to you, but that doesn't mean they're true. Push back, and have the last laugh. In the dance between you and your monster, choose to lead.

DOING THE WORK

Take a minute to picture your monster.
1. What is your monster's name?
    a. List three characteristics of your little monster.
2. What goals does your monster distract you from pursuing?
3. Sketch your monster, and hang it where you can see it.

CHAPTER 5

RUN FOR YOUR LIFE

A cop chases a burglar down the streets, through alleys, over all sorts of terrain. The cop thunders on, his job being to protect the community. But still, the burglar gets away. And he will almost *always* get away because there's way more at stake for him than for the cop in pursuit. Why? *Because he's running for his life.*

When you hit that field, cleats on, you need to run for your life. No matter how hard you work in those 90 minutes though, your actions outside of the game or practice matter just as much. You need to establish your priorities and eliminate distractions. Back in Chapter 3, I passed along the priorities I've identified for my team: health and well-being > family > career > soccer > everything else. You commit your energy and focus to the top of the equation and then sequentially work through the priorities.

This is in contrast to an increasingly popular concept of aiming for a balanced life. The classic work-life balance is often painted as the ideal. But the truth is that you can't win if every day has that perfect balance. *How can you reach your greatest goals if you aren't pushing against challenges?*

The most successful people will tell you that there are healthy extremes. You have to live in the healthy extremes of work, practice, and sacrifice to hit your goals and build up to the next ones—the balance of your life will come over the months and years, not at the day-to-day level. Now, I'm not here to validate player burnout—that's a fool's game with players viewed as cogs in the machine rather than living and breathing individual human beings. I am, however, advocating for players to push themselves outside of their comfort zone at the right time and place. Think of it this way: during pre-season training camp, you're going to increase your physical intensity in preparation for the season; you'll manage fatigue while building your longer-term capacity. During the season, there are extremes of workload, but they appear more during games, carefully balanced with extreme periods of rest and recovery between games and extreme sacrifices as there is almost no time for "everything else."

Active rest is deliberate rest and intentional regeneration. Time off is not time to celebrate and party; it's time for extreme regeneration. Players get days off from practice, but there are no days off from thinking and acting like an elite athlete. So, if you aren't physically training, you're tapping into physical, mental, emotional, and even spiritual regeneration. Time with family and friends, solitude, spending time in nature, playing with your dog, watching a sunrise or sunset, and staring at the ocean are all part of the process. The real trick is scheduling out when you'll be pushing yourself to healthy extremes or taking an active rest to heal your mind, body, and spirit. Do this deliberately.

It again goes back to priorities. I see my own performance as running on an eight-lane track. I want to stay firmly in lanes one and two—these are the fastest and most competitive lanes. I want to stay focused on winning games (lane one) and recruiting like-minded competitors for my team (lane two). Lanes three through eight are reserved for other tasks and priorities; it's in these lanes that you'll also find more distractions that have the potential to slow you down. Some people love floating in these lanes because it distracts from how slowly they actually operate in lanes one and two. It may be tempting to explore other lanes, but as you swing out into lanes three to eight, you will encounter more distractions that drain your energy and capacity to keep your attention in high-clarity mode. Running a lap in lane three will cost you 3.8 percent more energy. Lane eight? 13.4 percent. You certainly cannot win there. Be clear about what's in your lanes one and two. Stay focused on the prize.

Our world is full of distractions. Whether it's the buzzing of your phone, conversations by the water cooler, or a mental grocery list, distractions are always pushing closer and trying to become a core focus. If you stay disciplined and set on your priorities while identifying and eliminating distractions, you will achieve far higher outcomes in way less time. This is true for soccer and beyond.

Remember, we always have maximum attention, it's just a matter of where we allocate our focus. We often split our focus between multiple things: TV, texting, working or doing school work, petting the dog, etc. You can choose to eliminate all of those. Consider someone who studies or works from home—this is the biggest opportunity to accelerate your achievement and quality of life ... but it can be a distraction-rich environment too. Running for your life is about efficiency, prioritising, and removing barriers between you and your goals, whether that be excuses, distractions, or people who don't have your best interests at heart. Sometimes, *you* are your biggest barrier.

I can remember Mr. Chambers, my English teacher from Colchester Royal Grammar School. His clickety-clack shoes would announce his arrival as he scurried along the hallway to the classroom. I can hear him now, "You can do better, Juniper." At that time in my life, in most classes, I was happy doing "just good enough." I had the potential to be an A student in every class, but I was cruising along easy B street in half of them. Mr. Chambers knew I was slacking, and it drove him crazy. He always wanted me to be better. I was busy with soccer training, rugby practice, and riding my bike to the local pick-up games most nights of the week so I wasn't sure I could do much more. Looking back, I just needed to stay in lanes one and two long enough to finish the assignment with quality. It doesn't have to be more work, but it does require selective attention for a period of time. Sometimes you need that person or thing to push your focus to maximum productivity and results. I can't force players to reach their potential; it's a choice to not settle for good and instead choose to be really, *really* good. Ask yourself: where's the edge of my potential? Let's explore that—it's so much further than you can easily conceive. Push yourself to imagine your potential at the very limit of what your mind can see for you. Your potential lies beyond that horizon. Far beyond. There's more beyond the reef.

Believe it or not, winning itself can be a distraction. The enemy for athletes is not always the other team or competitor, it can be complacency. Overconfidence after a win or series of wins can quickly become arrogance. "We're winning because we're good." No, you're winning because of your hard work and sacrifices—you have to continue channelling that energy.

We train ourselves to think in the Now and Next. These are lanes one and two when the whistle goes. Rather than holding onto previous mistakes like a bad pass, a missed tackle, or embarrassingly scuffing an easy chance to score, we want to stay in lanes one and two of the game. Processing mistakes quickly is the key. The same is true of defeats. Our associate head coach, PJ, does a great job of processing defeats. When we review our performances after a lost game, he explains to the team how it's like salvaging an old car. You strip it down to its bare components: you preserve the good pieces, process the bad parts, and then move on. Player or coach, we need to have our fullest attention on the right now and what could happen in the very next moment. That's it. You have to nurture your mental skills to quickly process the inevitable mistakes. Extract the essential oil from the moment and discard the rest. Learn, grow, move on. Fast.

The same is true for managing the experience of wins and losses if we look through a broader frame of time. We take time to enjoy a win, but the next morning, we're back to work. Wins go into "The Box," a mental compartment, which sits on the top shelf at the back of a very dark and dusty storage room of your brain, secured by a large chain and padlock. At the end of the season, you can pull The Box out to reminisce and celebrate all your hard work. In 2010, we won 19 out of 24 games, losing only 2 games all year. The final loss was in the sweet sixteen of the NCAA Tournament. A golden goal in the second half of overtime. This was the year The Box was born. At the end of the season, my players handed me a real box stuffed with photos, articles, and messages about our successes. I stumble across that box occasionally and I love the reminder it gives me to compete in the Now and Next. Reminisce, enjoy looking back at the distance you have travelled, but if you want to win, get back to looking forward quickly.

We can broaden the frame of reference further and apply the same principle from season to season. Yes, our success is building a legacy. But each year is a different team with different competition; there's no helicopter that will pick us up and take us back to the top of the mountain, where we finished at the end of last season. We begin a new adventure; it's a fresh start.

There aren't the stakes of being chased by a lion or tiger, but if you don't run for your life, your goals and dreams will remain just out of reach. Establish Now and Next attention, compete in lanes one and two, and then apply maximum discipline and consistency.

This is running for your life. As a teenager, I had a bunch of part-time jobs. Few aspects of these jobs were inherently joyful, and I learned to bring that element myself. What they all had in common was a demand to perform a single task, over and over again, for long periods of time. I sold windows, pumped gas, plated meals at a hospital, and worked the checkout at a gas station and a large grocery store. I painted curbs at gas stations, washed cars, served champagne at weddings, flipped burgers at agricultural shows, and loaded beer barrels onto trucks at a commercial kitchen. I also worked in that same kitchen. I can remember having this huge sack of carrots placed in front of me to peel. It was more carrots than I'd ever seen in my life. How could I peel a sack of carrots so big I'd struggle to hug it? I knew I'd have to peel this mountain of carrots one at a time. It became a personal challenge: how could I most joyfully peel the carrots? I moved the radio close to my station, nudged up the volume, and immersed myself in the task. Wash, wash. Peel, peel, peel. Chop, chop. I stayed in lanes one and two. Fully immersed in the task with a joyful posture. On Saturday, wedding guests will be enjoying my carrots. My compelling vision of the future! I finished that mountain of carrots and, wouldn't you know, they brought another burlap sack of carrots over to me. How big was this wedding? Hendrick had a few things to say about that, but I locked back into lanes one and two—fully immersed, joyful posture, compelling vision of the future. Time flew by.

Build yourself a clarity of purpose, focus your efforts, and stay locked into lanes one and two. Fully immerse yourself in the task, and commit to a posture of joyfulness. Consider the compelling vision of the future, apply discipline to your execution of the task right in front of you, and move forward. One foot in front of the other. Breathe and repeat.

Julie Andrews sums it up perfectly: "Some people regard discipline as a chore. For me, it's a kind of order that sets me free to fly."[6] So channel your focus, use discipline to dismantle distractions, and run for your life.

DOING THE WORK

Imagine your life on an eight-lane track.

1. Identify what your highest priority goals are in lanes one and two.

2. What tasks and distractions do you have in lanes three through eight?

3. Spend a full day "running" in lanes one and two, and test your healthy extremes.

    a. Repeat every day for a week, and reflect on your progress.

LISTEN TO GRANDMA

When I was a boy, my mum would take my siblings and me to my grandparents' house every Tuesday after school. I don't know how it was possible for one person to bake so many cakes and sponges in a single day, but my dad's mother, my grandma, was a baking machine. And she did this every week. I had Cub Scouts meetings nearby, so as my mum took my siblings home, I'd stay for dinner with my grandma and grandad. She would hand-cut potatoes and fry them to make delicious chips. Then she would fry me a couple of eggs. Simple, but I was in heaven. I could taste the love!

As I wrote earlier, both sets of grandparents lived as young adults through the hardships of World War II. They experienced food scarcity and rationing for years, and I attribute that time to why my grandma showed her love with food. Grandma gave us more than nurturing and tasty treats though. She had valuable wisdom garnered through her years of life experiences that she was willing to pass on to us. Now, as an adult, I see the generational wisdom of our elders get too often overlooked. Our most senior citizens may not be well-versed in digital conversation, but if you're willing to stop, look up, and listen, it can only add a richer texture to your understanding of the world.

I was lucky enough to have all four of my grandparents in my life for a long time. Everyone lived in the same town, all within a few minutes of each other. They were always available for a chat, a laugh, a cuppa tea, or to pass along some nutritious, generational advice. My mum's mum, who we all called Big Nanny, had many sayings and aphorisms that she had learned from her mother, my Little Nanny. Little Nanny, my great-grandmother, lived into my early childhood years, and it makes me happy to think about those times being around multiple generations of our family. These kernels of wisdom continue to resonate today. Even though my grandparents are no longer here, I know their wisdom will continue to be passed down, from me to my kids and beyond.

Words of Wisdom

If I think about it, there are too many phrases from my grandparents and my parents to cover them all here, so I wanted to highlight a few that I find the most impactful.

There's no such thing as can't. This one was a staple of my grandparents. I can hear them saying it even now. Or as my Little Nanny used to say—*"Can't" is dead long ago, and "can" is still living.* If you accept something as impossible or unachievable, then you *can't* do it. But if you believe you *can* accomplish that far-off, distant goal, the dream is kept alive. It remains a possibility, and that's all it needs to be. I've always leaned toward positivity and optimism; it's part of my core belief structure for winning. It's crystalized in our team culture as what we call a no-limits mindset. *Why not us?* 🚀

Waste not, want not. I believe my grandparents put this to the test during the war. There was simply no option to waste anything; every resource had to be rationed out and used carefully. Food was never thrown away without thought in our house either. The Sunday roast was still delicious on Monday night and maybe in a sandwich on Tuesday lunchtime—roast beef with Grandad Clarke's homemade horseradish sauce, which would blow your head off. The principle is simply to maximise your resources, to not be wasteful because everything has value, down to a single nail or screw. If you ever needed a certain type of screw, piece of wood, tool, or bracket, you knew you could find it in Grandad Jake's shed. His carbon footprint was virtually zero, and "Reduce, Recycle, and Repurpose" was already a way of life.

Do as you would be done by. This is how my grandparents would have expressed the Golden Rule. Treat people with respect. Be kind. A simple expression of respect for our shared humanity should extend upwards and downwards through social hierarchies and across cultures. Effective teams need this to be a foundational principle, but the highest-performing teams also understand that an extension of simple human respect is respect for someone's life experience. Respect for a grandparents' wisdom is no different to offering an appropriate level of deference to a coach, a teacher, a team captain, or anyone in a position of authority for that matter. The nuance is in the power differential. In a locker room, this dynamic can make or break a team. Respect for a senior player's experience balanced with human-level kindness up, down, and across the room is a potent recipe for winning.

If at first you don't succeed, try, and try again. This is another saying I heard my grandparents say over and over. They were no strangers to perseverance. It's the fortitude to keep trying in the face of failure that really defines success. Get knocked down, get up. Stop feeling sorry for yourself. Figure it out. Repeat.

Worse things happen at sea! My grandparents would say this with the same cadence as "There's no point in crying over spilt milk." If you're really upset, it's a very comforting thing to hear that greater problems are happening at sea—what those worse things are, I still don't know!

An oyster needs grit to make a pearl. I grew up in England's oldest recorded town, Colchester, where you will find some of the world's finest oysters, which have been grown there since Roman times. There is an annual Oyster Feast dating back to at least 1845. Oysters layer minerals over a piece of grit or sand over time to create a pearl. A pearl doesn't begin life as just a really small pearl; it begins as grit, an irritant. In fact, grit has a very clear advantage over an inherent mini-pearl: grit has the bravery to get inside the mollusk and commit to growth over a long period of time. Be brave when jumping into unfamiliar experiences, unconventional adventures in life, or pathways for which there might not be family history. I'm happy to have coached a lot of first-generation college students. They can face a sense of imposter syndrome more than others. Slowly, the feeling fades and their experience aligns more closely with their teammates. They emerge with degrees, with advanced degrees, and springboard into the next chapter of their lives like everyone else. We are all grit in the beginning, full of imperfections. Be humble about that. The biggest mistake people make is assuming that, to achieve something, they have to start out as a mini-pearl.

Hierarchy of Knowledge

There are plenty of discussions that highlight the differences between boomers, millennials, Gen Alpha, Gen Z, and everything in between. Coaches may choose to lead emerging generations differently, and when it comes to the craft of delivering information, I tend to believe in adapting for your audience. It is hard to engage the full attention of our current players, and it's just as easily lost. They are used to vivid and engaging information delivered in smaller, deliberately-crafted units of information. As coaches, we should adjust our messages to meet those demands if we want to build a high-performing team.

The methods and styles of communication might need to evolve, but our core DNA really doesn't change. From my perspective, that means the message itself is no different today than when I started my soccer career.

Don't we all feel good when we are a better version of ourselves today than we were yesterday?

Most people look to be part of a community, don't they?

They get satisfaction when connecting with others, right?

Isn't there a sense of satisfaction we get when using our individually unique talents?

These core motivations drive much of our decision-making; they are pretty universal and carry through the different generations. Generational wisdom is so robust—that's why it makes sense to listen to grandmas, grandads, and our most senior citizens. Wisdom accumulates from the generations who lived before us, the current generation, and eventually, the generations ahead of us. By walking with open minds and hearts, we can discover and embrace new ideas.

True wisdom evolves when humanity discovers new information, not just new cultural trends, new celebrities, or a new social media platform. Equally, the hearts and souls of each new "gen" group don't change. They experience life through very different cultural, historical, and technological lenses, but they love to work just as hard as the group before them. I've often heard them called lazy, coddled, and entitled. I don't buy it. My job is to coach their DNA and connect them with the why.

If our culture is strong, I don't have to teach the same principles again and again as we add new players. The way we operate, our generational wisdom is passed down from year to year. Respect for one another and respect for the experiences of the "grandmas" on our team allow for an organic flow of knowledge vertically down through the team. I like to think it mirrors the natural world.

I'm reminded of a story about a pod of orcas who developed the specific hunting practice of flipping over under the water as they attacked a great white shark. With the shark in their mouth, they return to the right side up, and the shark becomes frozen, in a trance-like state: dinner. Marine biologists identified the behaviour in only a very small but distinct family of orca. The longevity of the behaviour proved it was passed down through the generations. Remarkable generational wisdom. Imagine the success rate of a new "gen" of orca who stopped listening to their grandmas. Equally, imagine the success rate of the orca family if the new "gen" stopped searching for new ideas. What happens if the older generations dismiss the new ideas out of hand? The vertical relationships of any team, family, culture, or organisation needs a healthy tension between generational wisdom and new ideas if they want to win in the future.

You do you. Not a phrase my grandparents would have used; they were from a time when individuality wasn't enthusiastically encouraged. They lived through world events that reinforced thinking as a nation, more than as an individual person. But, "You do you" is a phrase that gives permission to explore individual actions and decisions. This promotes a rich tapestry of cultures within cultures. I hope my kids continue to enjoy that freedom of expression.

A penny saved is a penny earned. This is something my grandparents told me plenty of times. Money was a finite resource for them and had to be squirrelled away for hard times later. You had to *take care of your pennies* with the promise that the *pounds would take care of themselves*. Yes, frugality should be practised, and this advice is mathematically accurate. While *money doesn't grow on trees*, it will grow with the right investments. As generational wisdom cascades through new generations, we should always stop and listen. We can respect the life experiences from which wisdom originates while also testing, challenging, and informing the global IQ as new understanding emerges.

Eventually, our players graduate into the professional world, and for many, that means professional soccer. Our players learn how an effective team operates with a healthy vertical tension, which is flipped upside down on them at graduation. From being the grandma in our locker room, they will progress to a new team, a new company, or maybe graduate school. They are the baby orca once again, and we hope they search out the experience around them, stop, and listen intently. We also hope they feverishly innovate. If we're lucky, they'll all visit us and share how they've taken the tools we've given them, combined them with the new ones they've acquired, and teach us how they have applied it all in their new lives.

DOING THE WORK

1. List three pieces of generational wisdom you remember from your grandparents.
2. List three people you admire who are not on social media.
3. Spend three minutes a day in deep reflection for one week, and document how it changed your behaviour.

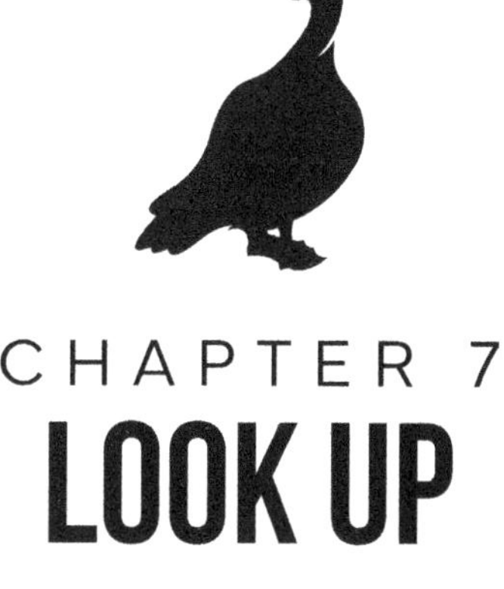

CHAPTER 7
LOOK UP

My sister once gave me a challenge: If you're ever having a bad day, put your hands in the air (like you just don't care), look up, and yell the word "joy" as loud as you can. I'm always up for a challenge, and what I learned was that it's very hard to feel bad when you take on that particular challenge. Thanks, Sis.

Physically, you are adopting a confident, chin-up, shoulders-back posture. It is also a practice of intentional engagement, mentally and emotionally, with the present. You see people doing the same thing on roller-coasters, at concerts, and at sporting events. Before the rise of the screens, being present was a natural way to engage with the world around us. We would share our lived experiences by describing what we saw, heard, and felt. More often now, people want to document the experiences around them with videos and photos. There's nothing wrong with capturing memories in video and picture form—I do it a lot. I'm suggesting that the selfie at the Grand Canyon is overrated.

The time taken to capture the perfect picture might be better spent just allowing the euphoric feeling of awe to overwhelm you. You can experience the Grand Canyon just like you can experience sports and life. Be deliberately present, physically, mentally, and emotionally. Look up, and nature will reward you. When I'm running, I sometimes catch glimpses of wildlife if I'm looking up. I've stumbled upon a bighorn sheep on the South Lykken Trail in Palm Springs, dolphins and the occasional whale at Crystal Cove, a bald eagle soaring over the Newport Beach Back Bay, and one resting on a light post in Washington, D.C. I once saw a particularly cheeky bobcat run through the middle of the UC Irvine campus—so many students were staring down at their phones, I think I was the only one who saw him.

Experiencing a sunset over the ocean, a mountain range in the morning, or an encounter with a wild animal offers up a soulful feeling that is exponentially different from looking at a picture of any of those things. No matter what is going on around you, if you don't look up, you're going to miss life.

Beyond the Screen

A cell phone. For many, that screen is the last thing seen at night and the first thing seen in the morning. Phones and social media offer countless rewards—connection, access to information, a tool to get from Point A to Point B. But for all their good, our phones and the content they carry create mind-numbing conformity of thought. They fill all of the important quiet spaces in our day. As a parent, I'm trying hard to be disciplined with my children's screen time, and it's tough. I find it hard to put the screen away myself. I've started leaving it in the car when I'm at my kids' sports and activities, and I try to leave it in a drawer before leaving for date night. Phones, computers, and the internet are tools, but they can't replace the real experiences of life. Screens are built to engage our attention to such a degree that our natural ability to reflect, be curious, creative, and innovative are stifled. These are your transformative thoughts. Pair that with algorithms that feed us information and content specifically curated for us and we lose out on exploring the world on our own terms—*we lose the ability to think for ourselves!* Online, so many people are trying to dominate your attention, influence your opinion, and tell you what you should think. If you're always stuck looking down, you'll extinguish your natural supply of transformative thoughts.

It's on my longer runs that I've recognized that if I clear away distractions for a sustained period of time, I experience more transformative thoughts—I call them my seven-mile thoughts. If I put away my headphones, turn off the music, send Hendrick off on a mission, there's nothing left to pull my attention away from natural, creative thinking.

Early on in a run, without external distractions, I experience a chaotic stream of consciousness, but that slowly gathers coherence, and around the seven-mile mark (or about one hour), my experience becomes really calm and reflective. Reflective thinking galvanizes curiosity, curiosity awakens creativity, and my mind explores new ideas, innovations, and solutions. I encourage you to find extended periods of time without screens or external distractions. It can be while running, walking, or even simply staring at the ocean. It's the extended time that really matters. Have you noticed how easily people's opinions of soccer games become eerily aligned with the half-time experts? Try watching a soccer game on mute and ignore the half-time discussion. Draw your own conclusions. Enjoy time without music or podcasts controlling your attention or the screen telling you to think the same things as everyone else. Enjoy independent thinking. Enjoy some time just being present. Enjoy learning *how* to think.

Flow on the Field

For an athlete, looking down is the kiss of death. Whether you're running, jumping, or throwing, if you look down at where your feet are, the next moment, you'll be looking up from the ground. When you're truly present, you don't even have to look—you're able to observe and process everything around you instantaneously. High performance is based on instinct, which is grounded in the present. This manifests in smooth, fluid, and natural movements. When your attention and concentration are so focused on the task at hand, everything else seems to just melt away, and time slows down. This is the concept of "flow" as coined by the psychologist, Dr. Mihaly Csikszentmihalyi.

Artists, doctors, engineers, and athletes can all access the flow state—anyone can. When you engage with challenges that match or slightly challenge your skill level, and you have a clear sense of the progress with immediate feedback, you open yourself up to being "in flow." This engagement creates a subjective experience where goal after goal starts to blend together into a smooth, timeless blur that ultimately feels satisfying. When you're in flow, you feel good—you're doing what you want to do with a sense of focus and effortless control.[7] But flow isn't achievable all the time; our attention is always challenged, externally and internally.

Dr. Csikszentmihalyi criticised why many people fail to achieve flow. He pointed out that many people prefer doing meaningful work over mindless downtime. Americans, however, have been conditioned to "hate their jobs and love passive relaxation."[8] At the time, Csikszentmihalyi was pointing a finger at the rise of television, but this extends to the rise of the internet and phone usage. Scrolling through TikTok or Instagram is meant to be easy and satisfy all our cravings for entertainment. This distracts from the perfect conditions for flow. Csikszentmihalyi said that we need challenge to tap into a truly joyous flow state:

> People seem to concentrate best when the demands on them are a bit greater than usual, and they are able to give more than usual… If there is too little demand on them, people are bored. If there is too much for them to handle, they get anxious. Flow occurs in that delicate zone between boredom and anxiety.[9]

Unlike decision-making, which is executed in the Now and Next, the execution of a technique or moment in the game you have practised a thousand times should be done in the Now. This is without conscious thought, by simply allowing yourself to execute action. Work to remove thoughts about previous mistakes or future consequences until you are existing in the smallest possible moment, and you can execute on auto-pilot. The smaller that period of time is, the closer you are to pure "flow." Once you start making judgments about where the ball is going or how an opponent moves, your sense of playing in the Now has to extend into the Next. We talk about playing in the Now and Next, which captures the instinctive autopilot moments *and* the rapid decision-making process we need. Decision-making requires you to evaluate possible outcomes which takes you just beyond the Now and into the Next. The time frame for that is still a split second, and it's where we have to practise being responsive, not reactive.

There's an important distinction between being reactive—immediately bouncing off of whatever emotion or moment is happening—and being responsive, which is key for high performance. "Response-ability" is the ability to respond to the many dynamic features of your environment without being distracted by emotions or outside factors. Beyond the immediate instinctive execution of auto-pilot actions, our first cognitive thoughts are often emotional reactions. These originate from a survival instinct and are characteristically defensive and protective. Players will turn away from what they perceive as danger. It lacks bravery. Our second thoughts, which appear immediately behind our first thoughts are sharp, competitive, front-foot responses. They are more brave and aggressive. If you're looking down, or if you haven't practised "how to think," you can freeze. You become limited to emotionally reactive first thoughts, and even worse, delayed third-tier thoughts, such as regret.

Being aware of the way we think, practising, training ourselves to think efficiently, and managing our thinking in high-performance situations are all opportunities to selectively focus attention. In soccer, a key moment might be a goal-scoring opportunity. Our minds are capable of focusing so selectively on such an important moment that we become aware of the rotations on the ball, its smallest movements on the grass, the texture of its surface, and how it connects with the smallest angles of our feet. We can be so visually and kinesthetically focused that we hear nothing.

Our sense of time is distorted as everything appears to slow down. Once you acknowledge that your mind can do that for you, you can practise it like any other skill.

In my early twenties, I bought a 1977 Vespa. I had it sprayed ivory and navy blue with a silver trim as a nod of the hat to my favourite soccer team, Tottenham Hotspur. It was a thing of beauty. Riding it through the streets of Bristol on a rainy day, I rounded a corner and my back wheel lost its grip on the road. In that moment, time slowed down. My brain naturally and immediately focused all of its bandwidth on what I needed to pay attention to for survival. It may have only been just a second or two, but I somehow experienced the loss of balance, the ridges of the tread of my tire bumping over the uneven texture of the road. I felt every loose piece of gravel and the slick feel of the rain between the tire and the road changing with every tiny bump. There were no distractions. I was calm, and I made the necessary adjustments to find the balance to come out of the corner.

My Vespa incident response happened instinctively, but I had experienced a deep level of focus the mind was capable of. Armed with that understanding, I learned that you can practise finding a deep level of focus and calmness on the pitch in high-pressure moments. You can't experience a full 90 minutes like that, but you can allow yourself to go there in the big moments. I used intentional imagery practice before, during, and after every practice session and match for the rest of that season. Look up, deliberately eliminate distractions, play in the Now and Next, and focus your efforts on "how" to think, not "what" to think.

During my Vespa era, I was playing for the University of Bath. I became the starting number 9 while I was earning my master's degree in sport and exercise science. My research was all about psychological performance in sport. I was lucky to be fully immersed in the research and application of those principles at the same time. I scored 32 goals in 28 matches that season, and we won a National Championship. Understanding the power of selective attention and the practice of imagery improved my ability to think clearly, play in the Now, and to convert far more than my fair share of chances.

DOING THE WORK

1. How much time is reasonable to be on your phone in a day?
2. Check your phone's usage info, and write down the last three days of screen time.
3. How much time would you like to reinvest in yourself and your personal growth per day?
   a. What would that give you back in a week? A year?
4. Spend a full 24 hours without your phone.

PJ Woolridge, associate head coach, is a vital part of our coaching staff. PJ is a high-integrity professional and an elite-level competitor. *Photo Credit: Sandra Velez-Lopez*

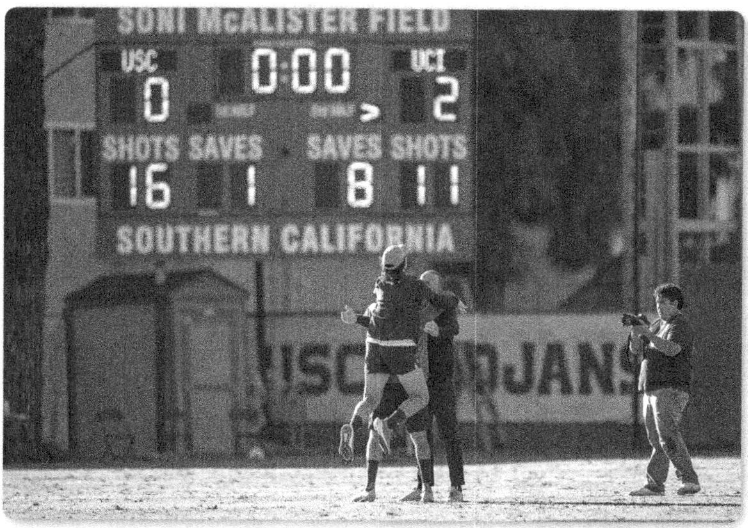

Danielle jumping on me and Ludo as the scoreboard flashes the final score in our win against USC. *Photo Credit: Sandra Velez-Lopez*

One of our adventures to the Grand Canyon in November 2009. From left to right: (back row) Mike Burns, Scott Juniper, Justin Neerhof, Makenzie Beahm, Kendall Fletcher, Rachel Schmid, Kellie Murphy, Caty Cope, Colleen Lopez, Milana Shabestari, Tanya Taylor, Christina Gorospe; (front row) Danielle de Seriere, Kim Horn, Erin Henry, Kim Conlan, Kathleen Lemieux, Kate Berrini, Frankee Kelly.

The team having fun before the second round NCAA game in 2010, before we beat Wake Forest 3-1. From left to right: #19 Sarah Busby, #24 Lani Amack, #25 Zuri Walker, #26 Raylean Robles, and #28 Amanda Hardeman.

The immortalized moment of the final whistle declaring a 1-0 victory over UCLA during the first round NCAA in November 2021. *Photo Credit: Sandra Velez-Lopez*

#25 Autumn Thompkins being pulled back by the jersey as #9 Alex Jaquez and #33 Glo Hinojosa watch in horror. *Photo Credit: Sandra Velez-Lopez*

The team in front of the Washington Monument in DC during NCAA tournament weekend in November 2021. From left to right: (back row) PJ Woolridge, Gianna Creighton, Kiera Smeenge, Amber Huff, Jenae Perez, Glo Hinojosa, Des Mendoza, Maddie Lauro, Autumn Thompkins, Suus de Bakker, Lilli Rask, Sophie Gillies, Scott Juniper; (middle row) Julia Gonzalez, Danielle de Seriere, Alex Jaquez, Piper Wurth, Chloe Ragon, Laila El Behery; (front row) Scarlett Camberos, Maddy Chavez, Destinee Manzo, Hannah Roberts, Mihaela Perez, Alyssa Moore, and Lindsey Huie.

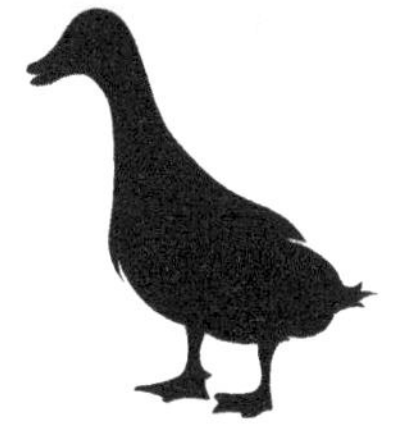

CHAPTER 8

WATERMELON COFFEE

About six months after moving to the United States, I was warming up a team for a game when one of the parents approached me. Cesar's mum. She kindly asked me if I'd like to try a "watermelon coffee." I instantly rejected the idea of watermelon coffee—I wasn't curious enough to explore such a confusing offer. My brain took what it heard and lazily shoved it through the first pre-existing pathway of understanding it could find. I politely declined. "No, thank you."

That interaction bothered me a lot, and it took me a long time to figure out why. It wasn't until weeks later that I finally realised she was offering me a *"Guatemalan coffee."* Maybe I wasn't fully engaged in listening, maybe I allowed my pre-existing conventions to win over curiosity, and maybe I didn't take the time to hear the soft Hispanic accent. It was probably a blend of all of these things, but ultimately I missed out on a cultural exchange and a lovely cup of coffee. And I *love* coffee.

My watermelon coffee experience became my personal reminder to stay open to new ideas, always check my rigid thinking, and choose curiosity over convention. Coaching in the United States exposes you to a rich array of international influences. I came from a country with a well-respected coaching tradition, but I've learned so much from so many people along my coaching journey here. Sometimes, because it's more comfortable, we hold so tight to our traditions and conventional wisdom that we blindly accept them and miss opportunities to connect, learn, and grow.

Equally, I don't jump thoughtlessly from one new coaching trend to the next in some fake race to stay ahead. We could fill a stadium with failed coaches who rode that train. Understand, your monster would rather stay comfortable doing things the way you have always done them. What he doesn't understand is that this path leads in a circle—right back to the same outcomes, over and over, again and again. The balance is to choose curiosity over convention but critically and thoroughly explore new ideas. Over time, your personal framework for success can expand to blend many ideas from remarkably varied origins. More powerfully, your surface area for future growth expands exponentially. Just like when you listen to grandma and explore generational wisdom, adopt a posture of humility when it comes to knowledge. Stop and listen. This requires you to look up, yes, but actually go beyond and critically challenge any preconceived notions you have. Assume that you have many. Push yourself outside of your comfort zone, and engage with somebody else's point of view. Embrace new ideas, and you'll unlock pathways to success you knew nothing about.

Conventions of Culture

When I was living in England, there was a well-established hierarchy of knowledge for soccer. It's a broadly accepted pyramid, with the English Football Association at the top. Founded in 1863, the FA, presumptively named as a global authority much like the Open in golf, is not only in charge of the rules and regulations of soccer in England but coaching education as well.[10] With a flow of knowledge from the top down, there's an established language and framework that allows everybody to work together. Having a common framework is really helpful and brings different ideas into a shared arena for discussion and testing. However, over time, that arena gets smaller and less welcoming. Those who teach and certify developing coaches need a rubric around which to evaluate and compare young coaches. The tighter the rubric, the better able we are to quantitatively compare the student coaches, but it comes with a steep downside. Coaches must contort themselves and their ideas to fit the established framework if they want to be certified and licensed. Ultimately you're left with a narrow concept of how to be successful in our sport.

When I took my first coaching licence test, the expectation was that your shirt would be tucked in, with socks pulled all the way up. And if you didn't, you failed. At the time, I didn't think anything of it. Everywhere I looked, I'd see other English guys running around the field with their socks pulled high and shirts tucked in tight. That's just the way it was. When I eventually came to the United States, the first time I walked out onto the pitch, everyone was looking at me: *What is this guy doing? Ninety-eight-degree heat and he has his socks pulled up and his shirt tucked in!* It truly was laughable to them. But at the time, I believed it was the standard dress for professionalism—eventually I broke from that convention and realised I could be a respected professional without sacrificing my comfort in extreme heat.

Having now lived in the United States for many years, I've seen how new ideas are more readily celebrated here. Instead of being considered "outside the framework," innovation is a cornerstone to success here. It is also true that the US has its challenges among established coaching education structures where rubrics inevitably conflict with innovation. I taught an online master's course in advanced soccer theories for 10 years, and the dreaded rubric made me anxious all the time. We need unconventional ideas to challenge the status quo, and they need room to breathe. Formal education doesn't always do that very well. For that reason, I lean more deliberately toward less conventional opportunities for development these days. I've learned that conventions are often disguised as wisdom. Knowing the difference will set you free. You might have noticed that there is some overlap in the content between the chapters in this book. Some similarities in the different ideas and concepts. Creating chapters that are completely sanitised of that overlap might make it easier to digest, but at what cost? The nuances of the ideas are what bring to life the reality of innovative thoughts—to try to divide them into isolated thoughts, reduce them to more clinical categories, is a shortcut to the mundane.

US Soccer has the same challenge as the FA: *How do you allow innovation to breathe* and *design a common framework for knowledge at the same time?* I wouldn't say they have the same issues as "socks up, shirt tucked in," but they wrestle with the impact that conformity has on suffocating ideas. Players and coaches are starting to more readily accept the idea that there isn't just one way to play soccer; there are many viable pathways. You have to explore what works for you, your team, your personality, and your environment. Innovation isn't about finding a single idea that works—it's coming up with a hundred ideas, and maybe one *really* works. Figure out what is at your core, and begin from there. This is what we have done, and will continue to do, on my team at UCI. As a result, we have an identity, but we aren't locked into a narrow vision of soccer or a rigid game model.

There can never be one solution to all the conversations in soccer. Just look at who has won the men's World Cup over the years—it's not just one team rising to the top over and over again. Instead, it's a mix: Argentina, France, Germany, Spain, Italy, and Brazil, just in the last six tournaments. Each country has its own unique identity within soccer; you can't get approaches that are more different than Brazil and Germany. In Brazil, soccer is an artistic expression of freedom embedded into the culture. Every player grows up with a shared feel for the game and an appreciation for their style. In Germany, the game has a more calculated efficiency, engineered for success. If both of these teams can win, it's clear that every soccer idea and culture deserves exploration.

As a college coach, I spend a lot of time recruiting. On one of those recruiting missions, I drove three hours to watch a high school game to watch one special player. She was a magical player with soft feet, a beautiful strike on the ball, and a next-level understanding of the game. I had tried to recruit her to a youth team a couple of years earlier but failed, even after talking on the phone with her brother to try and convince her to join my squad. There were many twists and turns, but the universe ultimately aligned, and she joined our team at UCI. I learned so much from Janelly about soccer and culture. She eventually joined my coaching staff and continued to influence the growth of our program. She taught me some tough lessons around the pool table too. At one point she started calling me "Jefe." I don't think she knows exactly how much I like that. Janelly and I couldn't have come from more different soccer backgrounds, but we figured out how to exchange ideas. She went on to play over 100 professional games and has represented Mexico as part of its national team. Janelly Farías still plays soccer and uses her platform to advocate for so many people and ideas. In 2020, she was invited to lead a talk at Harvard University on "Navigating the Borders of Gender, Culture, Language, and Sexuality in Sports and Beyond."

Soccer in the United States has so many different ideas, and each of us has the freedom to pull from any of them. There is so much space for innovation and exploration. Access to so many soccer ideas and cultures is especially exciting for me, a man from England who has come to coach in Southern California, seeing players and influences from around the globe. I never would have thought that I would have the chance to blend domestic players with players from England, Egypt, India, the Netherlands, Brazil, Ghana, Guam, Australia, and Japan. I've learned new things about the game from every one of them.

International Play

Before I hired my assistant coach, Danielle, she was one of my players. She grew up playing in Southern California and was on the UCI team for four years. She captained her team to the Sweet Sixteen of the NCAA Tournament in 2010 and still holds a lot of our goal-keeping records. After UCI, she played professionally in the Netherlands. The homeland of Johan Cruyff, Jill Roord, Dennis Bergkamp, and Vivianne Miedema. While she was there, her understanding of the sport grew in a number of ways. She learned about nutrition, sport science, and some nuanced ways to raise simple expectations of quality. Danielle knows how to stop and listen. She absorbs and understands cultures really well. She raised our standards for simply passing a ball.

It's not just getting the ball from point A to point B; it's *how* you're getting the ball there. If the ball is bouncing in—unacceptable. What's the texture on the ball when it arrives? What is its speed and direction? Most importantly, she learned that you are responsible for your teammates' first touch. Your last touch on the ball should take care of your teammates' first touch. Danielle de Seriere is now in the UCI Athletics Hall of Fame.

> *"Having the opportunity to play in Europe truly opened my eyes to the world of soccer. I was exposed to a completely different soccer IQ and played alongside some of the best players in the world who are still playing today."*
>
> —Danielle de Seriere (UCI 2007–2011,
> UCI Athletics Hall of Fame)

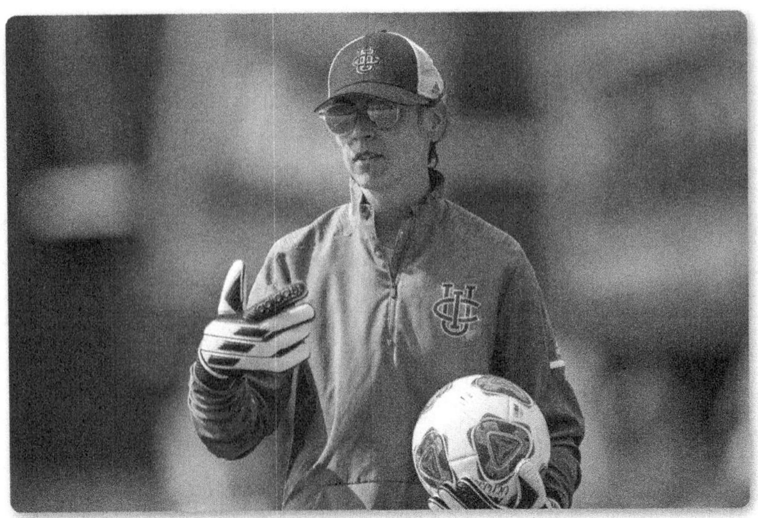

Our assistant coach, Danielle de Seriere, in August 2021 as we faced off with UCLA.
Photo Credit: Sandra Velez-Lopez

There are so many valuable ideas in the world that can be transformative if approached with an open mind. No matter where you come from in the world, you bring a unique perspective on life and the game of soccer.

Some international students who come to UCI are very quick to express their gratitude for women's sports being treated equally to men's sports. This isn't always the case in their home countries. During a first tour of our campus, one player saw our neatly groomed soccer pitch and said, "Wow, that pitch looks beautiful. Where do the women train?" That's a big moment to stop and listen. Reflect on that for a while.

Laila El Behery told me a story of taking a taxi to soccer practice in her home country, and the driver asked where she was going. As soon as she explained she was going to play soccer, the driver berated her for breaking societal norms and participating in sports as a woman. It's unfortunate that the bias in her culture was so strong that she had to experience that. It only emphasises the importance of their experience in the United States though. It offers international players an opportunity to eventually take their experiences home, influence their soccer federations, and support the growth of the sport in their countries.

"No one who has just gone with the flow has ever made a difference. When we step outside of the box we've been conditioned to stay in, we can break so many biases."

—Laila El Behery (UCI 2021–2025)

We learn so much from our international players, and they learn so much from their experiences here too. Wherever we travel, we find cultural experiences for the team, many times in place of a practice opportunity. Sometimes it's in nature, sometimes it's as much fun as we can find, and occasionally, it's a historical place. We have enjoyed waterfalls, sunsets, sunrises, hikes, and luaus in Oahu. We have floated on innertubes down the Boise River in Idaho and experienced a euphoric feeling of awe that overwhelms you at the Grand Canyon. We have ridden roller coasters together, played laser tag, and raced go-karts. We have visited Pearl Harbor, Monticello, the Washington Monument, presidential libraries, and the Civil Rights Institute in Birmingham, Alabama. Meaningful experiences can come in all shapes and sizes; you just have to be willing to engage with the world around you. Be patient enough to stop, listen, immerse yourself, and reflect on ideas that are new to you.

Growth experiences can happen across cultures but also across sports. My second sport growing up was rugby, and I still absorb new ideas and perspectives from my rugby friends. I love to work in a collegiate athletic department because I get to rub shoulders with exceptional coaches from tennis, golf, water polo, baseball, basketball, track and field, and volleyball. Seeing them practice and being close enough to see them coach in critical moments is amazing. We steal ideas all the time. We've copied sprint workouts to refine our running form and use volleyball terminology in crossing and finishing sessions, just two of many examples I could give you!

It's not just experienced coaches that you can learn from. In fact, some of the most impactful insights and the most elegant ideas can come from the most inexperienced people. The value of a fresh pair of eyes on my team is huge to break down our own ingrained biases. New staff are peppered with questions in their first few weeks for that very reason. At my kids' games, there are parents who are completely new to soccer but extremely accomplished in other areas of their lives. Their perspectives of how we do things in soccer are pure gold. The coaches working with the three to five-year-olds are some of the most creative (and patient) people anywhere across the coaching spectrum. I've learned from them how to teach ball-striking by imagining a face on the ball and how to defend using your arms like a seatbelt. Just last week, I learned how to protect the ball by acting like a penguin!

Whether you're offered a cup of watermelon coffee, advice about your sock game, or a penguin idea, stop, look up, and listen. Lean into cultural exchanges as precious opportunities to learn and grow. Do it all with humility and curiosity. You will be surprised what you learn, and I guarantee you will create a better, more innovative future.

DOING THE WORK

1. Can you think of an experience where you have made wrong assumptions about a person you just met?
2. If you are an athlete, which sports do you think you could learn from?
   a. Make a brief plan to observe and learn from that sport.

C H A P T E R   9

CLEAR EYES, FULL HEART

Twenty-something years ago, while still playing semi-professional "football" in the UK and coaching part-time, I published my graduate research on two little threads of performance theory.[11] That paper is buried somewhere in the dusty archives of a peer-reviewed journal called *The Sport Psychologist*. The original research was based on the data and insights of academy players from professional clubs in England and student-athletes playing at a highly ranked NCAA men's program. Some of those players progressed to the English Premier League, national teams, and one player even made it to the 2010 FIFA World Cup. It was a deep dive into how players' performances can be elevated or impeded by the actions of coaches along two very distinct dimensions.

The first dimension is the cognitive component, **role clarity**, which depends on the coach's effectiveness in communicating expectations. The second is the degree to which the player is fired up to do it, which is the emotional component known in the literature as **role acceptance**. Honestly, I found the process of scientific research to be a lonely experience and wondered if the work, which took me thousands of hours to complete, would ever really reach people who could use it.

That was until one evening while watching the NBC sports drama, *Friday Night Lights*, I saw Coach Taylor sum it up so nicely in his iconic rallying cry: "Clear eyes, full hearts, can't lose!"

The path to best performance requires "clear eyes," or maximum clarity of purpose combined with a "full heart," or that emotional feeling of being driven by every fibre of your being, from an energy source deep in your soul, to perform with everything you have. Sadly, Coach Taylor and I have never had the chance to sit down and talk it through, but I'm convinced we are on the same page. I've learned to use these principles as a framework to understand our players, our teams, and their performances.

Role Clarity

Building a high degree of role clarity accelerates in a high-quality learning environment. It's a measure of how well a player understands what they are being asked to do. Each player will absorb information in a different way according to their unique learning profiles, and it's a coach's job to meet these needs. Occasionally, I find a player who is wired identically to me. Those players listen, absorb, retain, and execute in the same way that I did as a player. Everything clicks for them. It's tempting to demand that everyone be exactly like them. In reality, for most other players, the "click moment" might not happen at the same point. It might happen in a classroom, for some it can be video, others need a walk-through on the field, and many will need repetitions in multiple modalities.

Tony Passey, from my time with him at the University of Bristol.

I discovered the power of role clarity with my coach at the University of Bristol, Tony Passey. I became Tony's captain on the field and eventually his assistant coach. I enjoyed the time we spent talking about the game, teams, players, and the people around the game. Tony, who spoke the Queen's English, was a man of great integrity and proper professionalism. He showed us new ideas on the pitch and was someone who fundamentally altered the course of my coaching career in the very beginning. He was an English gentleman with a big smile and a golden tan who was well-respected by everyone. Our Bristol team was a collection of hilarious characters. Talented players from different backgrounds, a lot of strong personalities, and a hunger for the game. Tony was in his seventies and managed to take this group of players and define a very specific method of playing. He did this by walking us through movements and positioning relative to the ball, again, again and again. He would repeat the central principles over and over until the repetition and refinement gave our chaotic squad a shared clarity of purpose. He used well-crafted language in the manner of an English language professor. He would ask us, *"Can you do a turn? And if you can, do you want to?"*

He was teaching us how to think. Each of us knew our role and, just as importantly, the roles of those around us. It brought a level of harmony in the way we played, and a level of accountability that high-clarity teams implicitly have on the field and in the locker room. My teams still play with a strong Tony Passey signature 30 years later.

On game day, in the fog of battle, that clarity can break down. Early in my head coach career, we were 1-1 with just a few crucial minutes left; the game hung in the balance. The movement of our back four was creating big issues, and I was screaming at them to drop quicker and deeper. It was a critical few moments. My centre back decided she had a few follow-up questions for me before she would execute the instructions. *When exactly should we drop? What if the player in possession is out wide? How far should we drop?*

I just needed an immediate response. I couldn't understand why she wouldn't follow the instructions and take immediate action. Our coach-player relationship was damaged in that moment. It took a lot of reflection, a personality profile assessment, and a long walk around campus together before the two of us began to understand one another. She was far from a disrespectful player—she just wanted to *understand*. She needed clarity in a different form. She had a thirst for knowledge, a need for a broader degree of clarity than others, and it was my job to give her that so she could play with clear eyes. The model of the game I was teaching was too restrictive. It didn't flex with the changing scenarios of a game. Sarah Devine, who played in back-to-back NCAA Tournaments for us, showed me we could be better. Role clarity emerges as you remove the barriers of misunderstanding, eliminate grey areas, and resolve conflicting ideas among players and coaches. Although it is a very cognitive process, the effect on physical performance is remarkable. Simultaneously, there needs to be role acceptance, which is a very emotional process.

Role Acceptance

Role acceptance is a measure of how emotionally "bought-in" a player is to the role they are being asked to perform. I've learned to appreciate that role acceptance and role clarity grow independently, requiring different nutrients, but they work in synergy during performance. Have you observed coaches who are perfectly good teachers without the ability to sell their ideas? Have you seen coaches who inspire people to produce effort without much tactical foundation? I've learned that both these coaching profiles will thrive in certain soccer environments, but they lack longevity. The coaches I admire the most grow both cognitive and emotional components in their players. Their teams play with clear eyes *and* full hearts consistently over the long term. Establishing a team environment where players are fired up to commit to their team, their club, the philosophy, and the coaches' ideas takes time.

There is a series of questions that I have learned to ask players to try and find their perfect roles. As early as the first meeting, I want to know everything about their nature: what makes them tick, their fears, what makes them feel excited to play, elated or inspired, and how they see themselves as athletes and people. On one recruiting visit with a potential transfer, it was clear that she had the ability to play anywhere on the field and was smart enough to understand any position. Role clarity wasn't going to be an issue. What did become clear was that she was falling out of love with the game; she'd been stuck playing as a striker when her nature was perfectly aligned with playing in the back line. She had been playing with clear eyes but an empty heart. A simple change of position was a significant ingredient in Coco Goodson's future success as she became a two-time All-American followed by a pro-career in Europe and the United States. Coco gave blood, sweat, and tears to UCI teams that won back-to-back conference championships and NCAA Tournament appearances. She did it with clear eyes *and* a full heart.

> *"I had completely lost my love for the game. I was frustrated because my strongest assets were my vision for the game and distribution. As a forward, those skills weren't being utilized to their fullest potential. With Scott recognizing and developing my strengths, I regained that love for the game, my teammates, and my coaches."*
>
> —Captain Courtney Rodenhuis, US Army,
> "Coco Goodson" (UCI 2010–2012,
> UCI Athletics Hall of Fame)

Coco Goodson hugging Devon Delarosa, who scored the winning goal against ASU in the 2010 NCAA first-round game.

Needless to say, I have tried lots of players in new positions since then and learned that not all scenarios are that clear-cut; the lesson is clear though: performances will *always* improve if the assigned role fits a player's true nature, not just what they're physically capable of. Sometimes, the chaos of the game demands that players have to play in uncomfortable roles. It is in these moments that you risk losing some emotional fire. If the game model for that player isn't broad enough to keep it burning, you need new fuel. The new role must be compelling, strategically important to the team, and needs to be filled by a special player. Players want to feel they are able to use their best strengths, be an important part of the team, and that their contribution has significance. All it takes is a coach who can understand those variables, ask the right questions, and take a long view of the process. Only then will players perform with full hearts.

My hope in pulling these threads of performance theory apart is to help players reflect and focus their performances through a different lens. Perhaps you will find a way to work through the frustration of not performing at your best, shift your perspective, and try a different way of thinking that might nudge you a little closer. If a football coach from Dillon, Texas (Coach Taylor) and a "football" coach from Colchester, England arrived at a similar conclusion, it tells me that, regardless of the variables of generation and culture, the highest performances come from a union of logic and emotion: truly the embodiment of "clear eyes, full hearts, can't lose!"

DOING THE WORK

1. As concisely as possible, summarise your role on your team.
   a. Is your understanding of your role deep enough and broad enough to handle the chaos of competition?
   b. Do you know your role well enough to teach it to someone else?
2. Describe what makes you more and less bought into your role on the team.

CHAPTER 10

THE WHITE LINE

The White Line. For most, it's simply the marker of when a ball or player goes out of bounds. But for me and the UC Irvine team, the line marks a moment of transformation. On game day, that White Line is the shift into battle mode.

Game days are special, so entering with the right mindset is essential. The team holds hands, taking a quiet moment of reflection as they prepare. This ritual of hand-holding is an expression of support between the players. Rudyard Kipling wrote that the strength of the pack is the wolf, and the strength of the wolf is the pack.[12] We need all of our individual players to be the biggest, baddest wolves they can be to strengthen the pack. We also need the team to work as one, with everyone supporting each other, which strengthens and emboldens every player. No one crosses the line until they're ready, until their focus is narrowed and energy channelled into kick-ass mode. And once they cross—there is only the game. Whatever may have been bothering or distracting them before is a distant memory left outside the White Line. By removing distractions and zeroing in on that White Line and your teammates, you can maximise the power of attention and focus.

Collegiate sports are distinctly more intense than at the high school level. The demands are measurably and observably different with players operating closer to a professional level. Any lack of focus or selective attention to the important elements of the game can be the difference between success and failure. Many players fresh from high school don't know how far their performance can go until they remove the distractions and establish a stronger mindset. The White Line concept helps our players to take control over their attention and concentration—many crossing over the threshold from high school to collegiate athletics.

Kiana Palacios played 67 times for UCI. She crossed the White Line with her teammates before every one of those games. Her ability to focus on her performances grew with every game during those four years. Kiana scored a lot of goals for us, and she had a huge impact on our conference-winning team in 2017. Kiana professionally played in Spain and currently plays in Mexico for Club America while also representing the Mexico National Team. I bought a front-row seat for her game against Brazil in the Gold Cup recently, just to see her play. I watched with tears in my eyes as she walked out with her teammates and crossed that White Line. It's hard to explain the feelings of pride I have for my former players. I'm just so proud of the player and person she has become. I watched as she sang her anthem, shook hands with the officials and her opponents, and rallied her teammates. Step by step, she prepared for battle. She is a wonderful player and brings a warrior spirit to her game every time she steps over the White Line.

 BE A DUCK

The White Line is a mental focus device that can extend beyond the soccer field. Anyone can use the concept of the White Line to focus their attention on a task, project, or event. When I visit elementary schools with Tim and Peanut Harper, I tell the kids they can apply what they know about focus in sports to their academics or anything else they want to do better. Do they wander into the classroom, or do they deliberately focus themselves and step into the arena? Before going into the classroom, when they step through the door, they should imagine there's a White Line in the doorway and make a commitment. Engage the same approach as we have with the soccer team, and learn to do that transition in an academic setting, applying the same competitive commitment in the classroom. This intentional engagement is what delivers results.

The White Line ritual was first implemented by my predecessor, April Heinrichs, when I was her assistant coach. Since then, we have performed the White Line ritual at hundreds of games. The players won't step across it to retrieve a ball or take a shortcut to the team bench. They fully understand the ritual's significance, and we talk a lot about other transitional moments we can use on game day to deliberately narrow our attention. It's not just the White Line now: all of game day is sacred, and the process of narrowing focus starts long before we get to the field. It can vary based on whether we are playing at home or away. There is always the moment you remind yourself that it is game day after waking up. As a team, we enjoy a meditation walk after breakfast, and a pre-game meal together. For me, it's also putting work away into a drawer, switching off the laptop, leaving the house, locking the door, getting into my car, and turning off my phone—all are moments for refining my focus and shutting out the rest of the world.

Back in my playing era, U2's Greatest Hits of the 1980s album was a big part of my transitions. The transitions through game day include auditory and tactile experiences along with the visual: Closing the car door and being met with a peaceful sense of quiet. Arriving at the stadium, where the noises continue to build. Heading to the locker room along the hallway where the texture of the floor changes and the sound of your shoes against it changes too. The smell of a freshly laundered jersey as you pull it down over your head like a superhero pulls on a cape. The taste of a sports drink. Feeling the change in temperature from the locker room to the field, the sun on your face and the breeze through your hair. . . . There's no flip switch for attention. You have to incorporate transition moments before your body, mind, and soul become engaged in the new task. We accomplish this by using imagery on a regular basis to complement our practice of transitions and narrowing focus. Twenty-four hours prior to a game, I will lead the team through a guided imagery exercise that includes some of these predictable transition moments. This solidifies the experience in their consciousness and reinforces a template of building mental fortitude and focus needed for the following day.

Carly Crowder was one player who really embraced the power of imagery practice and has mentioned to me years after graduation that it still resonates. Carly, now Dr. Crowder, was one of the hardest-working players we've ever had. She was a part of a magnificent UCI team that won

     BE A DUCK

back-to-back conference championships and 14 consecutive games, setting a UCI record.

"We used a lot of mental skills training at UCI including imagery practice. It turned out to be part of a great foundation for me in my career. I regularly use imagery in my preparation for surgery. Mindfulness, meditation, and imagery practice resonate more strongly with me as time passes."

—Dr. Carly A. Crowder, MD (UCI 2008–2012)

#13 Carly Crowder with the ball as we earned a victory against Gonzaga in November 2009.

Deliberately crafting your mindset is such an individual practice. There are stages we plan together, but the framework always has room for the individual. Some players like to be alone; they enjoy solitude and time for reflection. Other people need company to diffuse tension and nerves. Some people need a light-hearted chat, and others need serious talk. This accumulates in the moment when we come together before the game, becoming a pack, a true team. We all step across the White Line together. One or two players lead the final chapter in the huddle and draw it all together. Only then can we head out with clear eyes and full hearts, fully locked in.

DOING THE WORK

1. List the five transition moments that happen on your game day.
2. How does your focus grow every time you experience one of those transitions?
3. What is your final "White Line" on game day?
4. Do you think you are at your most focused when you cross it?
5. List five more transition moments you could add to enjoy your game day even more.

CHAPTER 11

SILVER-CAPED SUPERHERO

Photos of races like marathons always seem to capture the roaring crowds as the fresh runners bounce over the start line, and later, the bedraggled runners push through the finish line. But what about a few miles before the finish? The cheers from the sideline say, "You're nearly there, you look great!" No, I'm not, and no, I don't. I'm in the last stretch maybe, but I'm in a tunnel of pain right now, and I can't see the light at the end of it. More often than not, the people cheerleading have never run in a race or even trained for one. It's easy to be a cheerleader; it's harder to be a role model. As a runner, while I really appreciate the energy the cheerleaders give me, I prefer the support from those Silver-Caped Superheroes more. These folks are the people who have already crossed the finish line, are wearing those space blankets to stay warm, and have stuck around or are walking back down the course, encouraging the rest of us. Those are the remarks that resonate at a deeper level—that's where you can get a different bounce, feeling the pace and energy build deeper in your gut. I've never been a member of a running club, but it's amazing to see how they support one another. Members who are not in the race (but are clearly experienced) will jump out and run a half mile or so with their teammate. I get as close as I can because I want to soak up their advice too. They aren't telling the runner they are nearly there; instead, they are direct, positive, and optimistic, offering tangible, technical advice on *how* to get through the finish line.

We have to navigate the same dynamics on the practice field. For fitness training, we use the classic beep test that gets progressively faster—you may remember it as the pacer test from your gym classes. Same thing, different beeps. Well, the players who can't keep up stop first and assume the role of cheerleader once they get their breath back. It's great to support each other, but the last thing their teammates really want to hear are the voices of players who stopped early and now get to enjoy a good rest. It's a motivation killer at best and often becomes a disruption. I'm not anti-cheering, but there's a difference between an encouraging Silver-Caped Superhero and a cheerleader—a Silver-Caped Superhero's impact is just much more motivating. The voices I encourage are from those who are still running. Dragging each other from one level to the next, taking on the greater challenge again and again.

Our bench is high-energy across the board during a game. Everyone on the team is responsible for maintaining that energy, from our newest players to our seasoned athletes. Positive, optimistic voices have a collective impact on those still in the battle of the game, but the Silver-Caped Superhero concept is even more effective with the powerful voices of our experienced players. They have already proven themselves in our program and are benched for different reasons: short or long-term injuries, or for brief spells of rest. These are the players I look to most to use their voices. These veteran players are most impactful at delivering words of encouragement to players who are about to get into the game or as the first words for players coming off the field. Cheerleaders play a role too, but our Silver-Caped Superheroes are gold on the sideline and in the locker room.

Discipline Is a Super Power

You may remember the Julie Andrews quote from Chapter 5: "Some people regard discipline as a chore. For me, it is a kind of order that sets me free to fly."[13] I used to see discipline as something that teachers threatened me with if I didn't obey the rules. To be disciplined was to receive a punishment. Thankfully, swipes with the cane or rulers across the back of the hand were a thing of the past before I ever needed to be disciplined in school. I've stood against a wall, attended detention after school, and picked up a lot of trash though. At that point, I saw discipline as something that happened in response to my bad behaviour. It wasn't until later that I started to understand that discipline was a part of the set of behaviours that made winning more likely. Sports taught me that. I hated the disciplined environment in school, but I loved the discipline of sports. Rugby in particular showed me a whole new level of discipline. I loved to win, and sports connected discipline with victory for me much faster than Latin class would ever connect me to success in life.

The disciplined environment in my school mostly just supported ancient conventions and old-school methods. I certainly wasn't an ill-behaved student, but I nudged back against some of that nonsense. It all created some cognitive dissonance for me, and when you consider the Julie Andrews quote, you can see why.

How can discipline (interpreted as "restriction") provide freedom? One of the greatest challenges is rewiring the idea of discipline so you are eager for it. The lightbulb went on for me when discipline, which had always been done *to* me, became a self-discipline commitment. If you're disciplined about doing the right things for yourself every day, you have the opportunity for maximum freedom and potential. Your discipline makes you faster, stronger, smarter—like a superpower.

Measuring the outcomes of your discipline varies. It's fairly easy for running because it is largely based on quantitative measures. Am I running farther? Faster? More often? And the most important: Am I enjoying it?

Soccer team measures are far more qualitative. It's not just about who scores or successfully blocks an opponent's shot—it's a broad team effort to deny our opponents, control the ball, and progress through the lines and our zones to the goal. Our performance is the result of self-discipline within many hours of practice, but it has to extend to the hours between practices. Resting, refuelling, and regenerating can all be done with self-discipline. We extend that mentality to academics as well; we have a self-imposed deadline that's always two weeks ahead of UC Irvine's. If there's a UC Irvine deadline for submitting grades or transcripts or filling out a particular form, etc., it's understood teamwide that we move that date up two weeks and handle it early. We reserve formal consequences for extremes. We encourage self-discipline and point to the natural consequences as the best feedback. For example, I have never responded to poor performance in practice with running. Not once. The self-discipline of running is reserved for growth opportunities. Cognitive dissonance is removed. I would have thrived in our environment, and I see our winners thriving too.

The first stage of growth always begins with yourself. Lead yourself first. Be self-disciplined and sustain it for a long period of time. Then, when you're leading your team or the other people in your life, you can actually be an effective role model rather than just a cheerleader—a real life superhero.

At age 16, I was enjoying being the captain of Wivenhoe Town Football Club's youth team. I was playing with some great players; we were all really good mates, and we won loads of games. That year, I was called into the first team squad to play with the men. A couple of the lads were only a few years older than me, but there were also a few at the end of their playing careers. It was intimidating being around players with that much experience and playing at the semi-pro level. In certain ways, I learned more in my first two weeks in that team than I had the prior two years. I was a good local player, but I had no idea how to translate that to playing with men. I loved every minute of my experience with that team even though I lost a bunch of money in card games at the back of the bus every week.

That season was also my first ever experience with a "player-manager." Essentially, it was like having our head coach in a dual role. He would coach and manage the team and play at the same time. Steve Dowman was our manager.

He was a player with hundreds of professional games under his belt in the third and fourth divisions of the professional football pyramid in England. He had 20 years of playing in some of the toughest leagues in the world under his belt. He had scars on his head that were older than me, and I don't think I ever saw him lose a header. For perspective, in 1977, the year I was born, Steve was named Colchester United Player of the Year.

I can remember one game in particular when we were all sat around at half-time, feeling sorry for ourselves and pretty dejected by a bad first-half performance. It was freezing cold, and the wind was whistling through a gap in the locker room window. Most of the lads were sipping on hot tea from broken mugs, and the rest had started talking about plans for later that evening. Steve was the last one into the locker room. He slammed the door behind him and the whole room shook. The door was barely hanging on by its rusty hinges, but he had everyone's attention. There was fire in his eyes, blood pouring from a gash in his knee, and steam coming out of his ears, nose, and throat. I thought he was going to explode. In a way, he did.

Every breath sent a cloud of expletives into the freezing cold air. It was a volume and intensity I had never experienced before or since. Mugs of tea flew across the room. Nobody moved and I was scared to death. I have no recollection of the final score and that doesn't really matter. What I do remember is how I felt. Among other things, Steve challenged my commitment, my bravery, my courage, and my discipline. It was like he had jumped inside my soul and beaten the crap out of all of my excuses. Our Silver-Caped Superhero, Steve Dowman, had demanded a warrior performance from us—and he got it. Bodies on the line. He had been there and

 BE A DUCK

done that his whole career, which gave him his silver cape and the power to demand it of others. I played my heart out.

A few years later, I played for another hybrid "player-manager." At the University of Bath, we had a coaching team comprised of Ged Roddy MBE, Paul Tisdale, and Ivor Powell MBE. Ged was in the more traditional role of team manager and is now a high-performance expert with FIFA. Ged was light years ahead of his time in the way we were organised. Then there's Paul, who previously played for Southampton in the English Premier League and was the "player-coach." Paul would train and play with us, and when he did, the level went through the roof. And finally, Ivor, who is in the Guinness Book of Records for being the oldest working soccer coach having continued working into his nineties. Ivor was unbelievable. He even represented Wales and played for Aston Villa in a career that spanned 1937 to 1954. When Ivor said anything to you, it felt like his soul was talking to your soul in a Welsh accent rolling with a vibration that hit you at your core. There was never tea flying across the locker room at Bath, but it was a trio of Silver-Caped Superheroes with high expectations and the experience to back it up. Each of them had been there and done it—there and back again. I was a good player when I arrived at Bath, but I played way above my station for Ged, Paul, and Ivor. We won a National Championship.

> *"Aggression, determination, the will to win. These have always been my watchwords, and they still are. That's what I try to instil into these youngsters. And they listen, they really do."*
>
> —Ivor Powell, on his philosophy,
> to *The Independent*[14]

Ivor Powell, MBE, who holds a place in the Guinness Book of Records for being the oldest working soccer coach, having continued working into his nineties.

What I learned from these experiences was that if I wanted to be a successful coach, I needed to inspire players to commit way beyond the Xs and Os. I was committed to showing my players that I was prepared to do everything, and more, that I was asking of them. I needed to connect and inspire on multiple levels if I wanted our time together to be transformative. These guys helped me experience a glimpse of what it felt like to be a part of such a powerful coach-player relationship.

I've committed to continuing my coaching education across the board—traditional licensing and professional development wherever I can find it. I've built on my sports psychology background to include meditation, mindfulness,

  **BE A DUCK**

and wellness. I became certified to teach strength and conditioning at the NCAA D1 level, and I recently spent time in Spain learning about their practices and principles of the game. I want my players to be just as committed to growth.

They need to prioritise fitness and well-being. They know I run. I spent years running everything with them, and although I work out on my own now, I've passed every fitness test I have ever asked them to pass. As I get older, I will adapt as necessary, but the principle remains. If I demand big things from them, I better stay focused on setting a good example. I'll keep running those half-marathons.

In 2021, I progressed to training for a half-Ironman. A few weeks before the race, I flipped my road bike, smashed my collarbone, and broke both my wrists. The Ironman didn't happen for me, and I returned the bike—it was a loan from that duck farmer I know! I had missed the race, but the determination remained. Get over myself and attack the recovery, just as I would ask of my players. I retired from the bike but kept swimming. I swam 100,000 metres last year. I remotely ran the coastline of Wales with a group of lads within the calendar year before that, an endeavour that totaled 810 miles. Who knows what I will do next year—the possibilities are endless.

Being a role model isn't about perfection. Part of the human condition is imperfection by design. That's one of the reasons we don't have traditional team captains. It's pretty unusual, especially at the collegiate level. On our team, everyone is expected to step up and give their all and lead when they see an opportunity. It's one way we have successfully hurdled common wisdom and the conventional guardrails around us. Now, we have more leaders, more leadership than we have ever had in the past. Because *everyone* on the team steps up. They're all on the path to becoming Silver-Caped Superheroes.

DOING THE WORK

1. Which personal achievements give you Silver-Caped Superhero status among your peers?

2. In one year from now, how would you like to answer that question? In two years?

DROP THE ROPES

Imagine if every relationship in your life was a rope. You're holding onto one end, and the other person is holding onto the other end. To communicate properly, there needs to be a healthy amount of tension on that rope—just like the string connecting two cans in a tin can telephone. The string has to be taut for vibrations to pass through. All healthy relationships have a bit of tension to them. As we grow older, meet more people, or enter leadership positions, you start to accumulate more and more ropes—and you're left wondering which ropes are actually important. The changing tension on both ends of those ropes creates disharmony.

With our team, we practise an exercise focusing on the relationships just in our locker room. Student-athletes are in a microcosm of life; school offers a testing ground for growing and building diverse relationships with other students, coaches, and professors, all while maintaining your relationships with friends and family. Specifically for the soccer team, there's a mathematical equation to map our relationships:

(30 players total x 29 players) ÷ 2 = 435 unique relationships

There are 435 unique relationships between all the players on our team of 30 young women. That's a lot of ropes everyone's holding onto. And the exercise helps the team visualise it.

We have everyone sit in a circle around the locker room, and someone holds on to one end of a ball of yarn. They pass the yarn ball to someone across the room, who then holds on to a point on the yarn and continues to pass the ball. Soon, a large interconnected web of yarn is built between the entire team. We ask the team to pull until they find healthy tension, and this visual representation of the team extends between them all. It represents 435 relationships, and you can see, if one person is pulling too hard or not hard enough, all the other relationships are stressed, or the yarn might just break. The tension warps the web. At the end, we cut up the yarn, and everyone ties a piece to their bag as a visual memory of what their relationships are all about. The idea is that we continually invest in relationships and don't take them for granted. Each of them is a living thing worth taking care of. A little bit of conflict—and healthy tension—is good. A back-and-forth between friends, family, and peers can allow for the spread of new ideas and the growth of relationships. More often than not, tensions arise because two people who are caring are both trying to solve the same issue but with different approaches.

Healthy tension only works with trust and support though. When that tension grows and the rope you're holding onto gets yanked in one direction, you might be inclined to yank back. Now, you're in a tug-of-war. In a normal game of tug-of-war, it's a few seconds of combative tension until one side yields. With relationships, that tension can grow for days, weeks, or months. Tug-of-war isn't collaborative, it's extremely adversarial. Both sides may have their reasoning, but it's a battle of will (or power). Sometimes it's worth that extra tug and heels dug in, but usually, the fight is fruitless. That's when you drop the rope.

It is useless to waste time in conflict with people who don't align closely enough with your mission; they will remain on the other side of that rope, tugging away, until you give up. And if you aren't careful, sometimes you're the one initiating that tug-of-war.

I used to struggle holding onto so many ropes, fighting every battle at the same time. I used to think that I had to precisely align everyone with my mission if I was going to win. That mental proposition required that I pull everyone across the line to my side, my viewpoint, and my specific mission. Instead of focusing on lanes one and two, I was trying to win in *every single lane*. That meant my focus was pulling on every single rope: with my coaches, administrators, support staff, our sports medicine team, the sports performance crew, literally everyone who was inside and outside the building. It was a major energy drainer. Entirely inefficient. Once I learned to drop the ropes, there was no more conflict—other people can keep pulling, but once there is nothing to pull against, the ropes fall pretty fast. I refocused everything on making progress in the lanes that I actually need to be running in. I was holding just a few key ropes. To be clear, everyone I work with prefers to win. They might not be wired precisely the same way that I am or want to operate exactly the same way that I do, but they certainly prefer to win than lose. They have their own set of ropes. Administration and support positions have 18 ropes representing our different sports and our team is just one of those.

By dropping the rope, you are free to build efficiencies, identify your real goals, avoid distractions, and run for your life.

When you are part of a team, there's the potential for tension in every relationship. Different personalities, varied approaches—it's a recipe for conflict if not correctly managed. Sometimes you need to drop ropes and reset. A dropped rope can always be picked back up, but you have to make sure you aren't pulling too hard OR being pulled around. The object isn't to win a tug-of-war; it's to share experiences with someone on the other end of that rope. When two people are working well together, there is a healthy tension on the rope reflecting a shared respect of the missions at both ends. There will be overlap in the scope of the missions but to expect perfect alignment in every situation is futile.

With a whole network of ropes in a team, it's my job to stress test these ropes. I want to apply tension and see how the team responds. And if I find that sweet spot of stress and tension, I can watch the team respond and grow. If I don't keep that tension, we risk moving backwards in our development. A slack rope can be just as dangerous as a taut one; no tension means everyone is pulling away from one another in different directions and at different speeds. Even during moments of high tensions with players, sometimes the best thing to do is momentarily drop the rope. If I have a player frustrated that they aren't playing, instead of yanking hard on the rope, we both need to drop our ends—and go for a walk. You don't have to be at either end of the ropes to solve a problem; you can benefit by simply walking together in the same direction and having a conversation together. Establish a shared mission and end-goal. Agree how we're going to develop them into the best player they can possibly be to find that opportunity for them to play. Only then can we walk back to the ropes and pick up our ends. Healthy tension.

You have only got two hands. Life has so many distractions, and if you're juggling ropes, you'll often miss out on accomplishing what's really important to you. When you feel that unhealthy tension, either from you or someone else, don't be afraid to drop the rope. For my team, when we're together, we don't have room for too many ropes pulling us around when our goal is to win games. Manage a healthy tension in your life, and focus your attention where it matters: accomplishing your goals and reaching your dreams.

DOING THE WORK

1. What is a source of conflict you cannot resolve?
2. What areas of conflict are in your life that drain the most of your energy?
   a. Which of those would end this very moment if you dropped the rope?

CONCLUSION

When a winter storm is crossing the Great Plains towards a herd of bison, they don't run away from it—they head right into the storm. It may sound unsafe, but instinct drives them into the inclement weather because if they were to run away, they'd be trapped in the storm even longer. Their fur is heaviest at the front of their bodies, and their wide heads can act as shovels against the snow.[15] Their strengths allow them to survive one of the harshest environments head-on. Amongst all my analogies and metaphors, I have a final one for you: posture like a bison.

Prepare yourself for the inevitable challenges ahead of you. Brace for the storm and attack it before it attacks you.

It's like when you're swimming in the ocean and a wave is heading right towards you. You can try to swim away and get swallowed by the wave. Or, you can head straight into the wave and dive underneath it. When our team is running beep test intervals as part of our physical development, they are waiting for the starting sound to begin at each level. There's a brief moment of time that it takes for that beep to start and finish; our players try to make it off the line immediately, right on the "b-" of the beep. The more fatigued you are, the more likely you'll be starting on the tail end of the beep. Fight that urge to delay, and attack instead. With the right posturing and preparation, you should be able to tackle anything in your path with speed and ferocity.

All of these methodologies and ideas I've presented in this book are going to help you create the strongest posture and a greater sense of control, confidence, bravery, focus, and fun. And when that all comes together, amazing things will happen.

In 2021, UCI's Anteaters played UCLA's Bruins in our first game of the year. We were down 3-0 in about 20 minutes—it was pretty bad. We won the next 70 minutes, 1-0, but, of course, the game was lost. We went on to win a conference championship and were matched up in the NCAA tournament against UCLA. Because of our 3-1 loss earlier in the year, no one gave us a chance. We were ready for it. Our posture was stronger. We were ready to go on the "b-" of the beep. It was before that NCAA game that someone took a picture of me smiling. A huge smile. Pretty sure I had the pink socks on. We had a remarkable level of confidence in our ability to win the game against a team who were, at that point in the season, undefeated. And we won.

We came back to the NCAA tournament in 2022 after back-to-back conference championships, where we were matched up against USC in the first round. Everybody who was talking about us was having some lighthearted fun about what we'd done the year before—sure, it was impressive that we took down UCLA, but the majority considered us lucky. It wasn't luck; it was work. Uncommon and extreme work. We had no days off; we worked hard, maintained the strength of our culture, and prepared our posture. And we beat USC.

By the time we arrived at the NCAA tournament in 2023, the conversation surrounding UCI had shifted. We could feel the cognitive dissonance in the world of women's soccer: *If it wasn't luck that carried UCI to victories over UCLA and USC, is*

UCI able to pull this off? When the NCAA announced on the TV who would be playing in the first round, we could already feel the inevitable match-up in our bones—UCI would play UCLA. The predictable script is repeated everywhere across sports in that moment. You jump up and cheer like you've won the lottery, and the social media team does their work. Our team was different that day—the jumping and cheering didn't last long, and we quietly grabbed our bags, thanked everyone, and walked out of the room. It was time to *train*. We had a week of preparation ahead of us.

UCLA was the number-one team in the country at this point. They had only lost four games in three years and hadn't lost a home game since November 12, 2021, when we beat them. For the 2023 NCAA tournament, we would be playing on their home turf again. People were saying that lightning couldn't strike twice for us. But we weren't listening. In our locker room, we were getting ready to head into the storm.

During our team meeting that Tuesday, I wrote at the top of our whiteboard in the locker room, "www.NCAA.com." I said to the team, "This is the homepage to the NCAA website. I want you all to imagine what the headlines will be on Saturday morning after our game on Friday night." The team threw out ideas and created a story of how the game was going to unfold. Our goalkeeper would receive her 31st career shutout. Our striker would score the key goal. And they wrote it all down on the board. This crystalized all the details of the team's visualisation of the game. Our posture grew stronger.

On Wednesday, we had our last team meeting. On a whiteboard next to our NCAA.com story, I wrote out, "How do you take down a bear?" I asked the team how they would fight a literal bear, not just the UCLA Bruins.

"We're gonna punch it in the face, coach!" they shouted back.

"So you're just going to run up to a bear in the woods, and punch it in the face? How's that going to work out for you?" I asked.

"Yeah, good point—the bear's gonna eat me."

"What else can we do?"

Soon, everyone was jumping in.

"You can't just punch it in the face once!"

"We have to punch it in the face together!"

"Don't stop!"

"Never give in!!"

Soon, our story of fighting a bear had become about a team of rabid anteaters jumping a bear in the woods. You can't just start a fight; you have to stay in the fight—and finish the fight. I said, "That's exactly how we're going to do it. I'll see you all on the bus in five minutes. Let's do this."

We travelled by bus up to our hotel in Los Angeles. We practised our normal routines: having dinner together, no phones, reviewing all our game plans, going over the Xs and Os. The storm was bearing down on us, and we were heading straight into it. Just like wind and snow whipping in a bison's eyes, I told the team not to be intimidated by all the national championship banners hanging on UCLA's campus. They're not really bears—they're humans. And it didn't matter what uniform they were wearing because no matter who we're playing we will never, ever, ever give in.

The next day was game day, and I could feel the fun coursing through the team. We enjoyed a meditation walk after breakfast. When we leave the hotel for our pregame meal, I often find myself gauging the mood of the team. On that day, their body language as they jumped on the bus and the energy in their voices told a story. They couldn't wait. We headed to Whole Foods, and I watched as the team walked around the store grabbing sushi, turmeric shots, and a rotisserie chicken. With the game just three hours away, you couldn't tell that the team was about to take on the number one team in the nation. They were laughing and joking around the store. But with every White Line we crossed—from the hotel, to Whole Foods, to the bus, stepping off the bus, to the stadium—our team's focus and posture only became stronger. Distractions melted away. I watched our players walk around the whole field, being very careful not to cross the white lines on the pitch. The team has many rituals: chants with lockers, desks, and tables turned into drums. Each ritual is another White Line: a tactile, visual, physical, and auditory threshold that is crossed together as a team. Our alumni from years ago would recognize it all.

Yet I never saw the fun leave their eyes. It never goes away; it just morphs into something more fun. The energy of the day started at breakfast, grew on our walk, and through Whole Foods. It was carried like an ember from a fire off the bus, around the field, and into a locker room. It arrived on the sideline and eventually onto the field where it became self-sustaining, burning hotter and hotter. Fun doesn't stay in the locker room, replaced by serious work—it morphs naturally into a deep sense of joy. A joy we are fully immersed in for the game.

I had one final whiteboard moment with the team before the game started. We had discussions all week, so everything on my game day whiteboard reiterated those main points. By then, I was just pushing buttons and lighting little fires. Their roles were already clear to them, and their hearts were full of fun and passion for the game. They had an aggressive game plan with control over decisions to pivot in the chaos. We were not undefeated, and we were far from perfection. But we would be brave. We would be relentless. We were never going to back down. We were playing with our UCI DNA. And we always face the storm head-on, with clear eyes and full hearts.

As I was talking to the referees, our team lined up on the white line and held hands. The pre-game ritual always starts with a moment of silence, so it's jarring sometimes for people who have never seen the team cross the White Line. There's a palpable feeling in the air. I always pause and stop talking to give our team the moment they deserve. Then, I watched them step across the White Line together—and it was on.

The game went exactly how we expected it to. We saw the storm coming, and we barreled head-first into it. We were defending more than they were defending. The longer it went on, the more it crystalized that this was how we were going to win this game.

When half-time came around, no one had scored. In our talk, I told the team, "I can't guarantee the outcome of this game, but we are not leaving here until we've scored." There was a healthy tension between the coaching staff and the players. They trusted us, and we trusted them. The team remembered what was written on the whiteboard: the story for the NCAA website. It was predetermined. That didn't mean it was going to be easy. We were in the eye of the storm and would need to fight through to the end. We went for it.

In the 72nd minute of the game, our central midfield player got a second yellow card, which equals a red, and she was sent off. In the last stretch of the game, we were now a player down, 10 going up against 11. Yet, amongst this chaos, there was still clarity. As my coaches and I stood on the touchline, having a brief conversation about how to reorganise our players, we looked up—the players had already adjusted their positions according to plan. We hadn't even finished our conversation, but the team was in a flow state, moving beyond the coaching staff's speed. It was seamless. It wasn't perfect, but they moved the right players into the right spots to give us the best chance.

At the 87th minute, we were still 0-0. We got into their half of the pitch, gained possession of the ball, and did well enough to earn a free kick 40 yards out from the goal. Our centre midfield maestro looked at our assistant coach on the bench for guidance on where she should put the ball. He gave a signal, and she nodded, but we weren't sure if she understood him. The stadium held its breath. She struck the ball really well, sending it into a dangerous spot about 12 yards from goal. The rest happened just like it was written on the whiteboard earlier in the week. The ball hit both posts before finally resting in the bottom corner.

Our team went nuts. Our fire was blazing. Statistically, you've won the game at this point; there's just three minutes left. We also knew that the scoreboard meant nothing until the time read 90 minutes. UCLA immediately lined up a pack of substitutes to throw at us for the final three minutes. What followed was some of the most phenomenal defending I had ever seen. Our players were responsible for the final outcome. You could see the bravery as they fought to hold onto what they worked so hard to earn. It's incredibly difficult to be aggressive and brave when you are emotionally, mentally, and physically fatigued. There's no room for error. You can't freeze; you stay in the Now and Next, anticipating and responding. We were running for our lives as a team, and we stood strong until the final whistle.

We had won.

If you go into our locker room right now, we still have "NCAA.com" written on the whiteboard. There are a few smudges and accidental erasures, but all the things we wrote down are still there. And they all happened. Recent recruits have been able to see this feat of visualisation and manifestation when they first enter the locker room.

All of the culture. All of the tools. All the button-pushing that I try to do for my team is to prepare them for those moments when it's not me—it's them. They're the ones out on the field. They're the ones risking it all over the course of 90 minutes. I've seen many incredible women grow up during their time at UCI and become better students, soccer players, and humans.

If you're reading this, you might not be a soccer player, simply someone striving to achieve your own goals. Building yourself up with a strong posture. No matter how big that storm rolling in is, anyone can be their most successful self.

And it all starts with that first lesson: be a duck.

Celebrating the final whistle at the 2019 UWS final in Calgary with Natasha Kai.

A celebratory moment of our win as the 2019 UWS National Champions. From left to right: Hillary Beall, Jayma Martin, Brianna Westrup, Arlie Jones, Genessee Daughetee, Taylor Kornieck, Chelsey Patterson, Natalie Jacobs, Maddy Vergura, PJ Woolridge, Scott Juniper, Jenna Nighswonger, Jordan Marada, Nicole Molen, Natasha Kai, Jordan O'Brien, Sonest Furtado, Natalie Ward, Catarina Macario, Madison Louderback, and Olivia Athens.

Standing with PJ, our associate head coach, holding the trophy as 2019 UWS National Champions.

#24 Maddy Chavez, #12 Kiera Smeenge, #33 Glo Hinojosa, #22 Destinee Manzo, and #16 Alyssa Moore heading straight into the storm, focused and locked in for the game in November 2021.
Photo Credit: Sandra Velez-Lopez

#12 Kiera Smeenge, our Silver-Caped Superhero who was sidelined because of an injury, high-fiving Piper Wurth (left) to celebrate a goal in our game against UCLA in August 2021. *Photo Credit: Sandra Velez-Lopez*

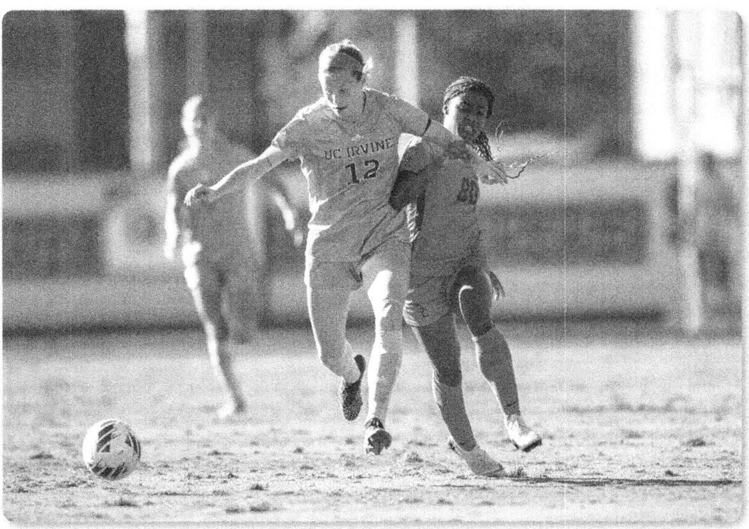

UCI player #12 Kiera Smeenge holding off #88 Simone Jackson during the 2022 NCAA first-round game. *Photo Credit: Sandra Velez-Lopez*

The team celebrating the winning goal vs Cal in August 2022.

Laila El Behery stepping off the bus, locked in and ready to challenge UCLA in 2023.

#30 Laila El Behery skipping past a UCLA defender who is on the ground.
Photo Credit: Sandra Velez-Lopez

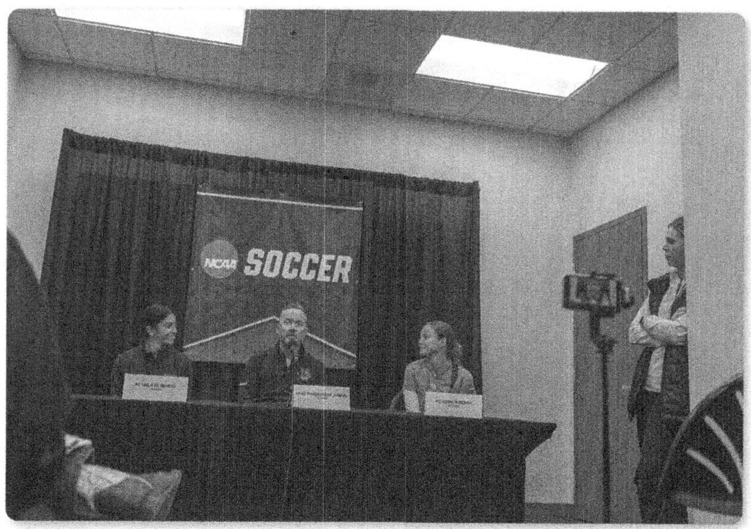

Having fun in a press conference with two athletes (Laila El Behery and Kiera Smeenge) in November 2023 during the first-round NCAA.

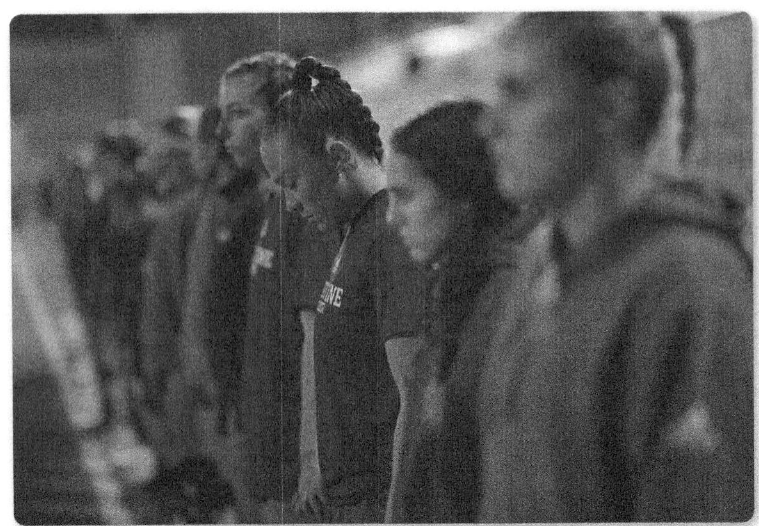

The team readying themselves for the game as they prepare to cross the White Line.

Alyssa Moore after scoring the winning goal against UCLA in November 2023.

Celebrating after the win over UCLA in November 2023.

Junior Gonzalez strategizing with me during a 2003 game.

NOTES

1. "Never Give In, Never, Never, Never, 1941," America's National Churchill Museum, accessed June 2024, https://www.nationalchurchillmuseum.org/never-give-in-never-never-never.html.

2. "The Story Behind 'Keep Calm and Carry On'," University of London, accessed June 2024, https://www.london.ac.uk/about/history/history-senate-house/story-behind-keep-calm-carry.

3. Clive Gilson, Mike Pratt, Kevin Roberts, and Ed Weymes, *Peak Performance: Business Lessons from the World's Top Sports Organizations* (New York: HarperCollins Business, 2002).

4. Plato, *Dialogues of Plato,* trans. Benjamin Jowett (Cambridge: Cambridge University Press, 2010).

5. Bart Geurts, "Making Sense of Self Talk," *Review of Philosophy and Psychology* 9, no. 2 (December 2017): 271–285, https://doi.org/10.1007/s13164-017-0375-y.

6. "Julie Andrews Quotes," Brainy Quotes, accessed June 2024, https://www.brainyquote.com/authors/julie-andrews-quotes#:~:text=Some%20people%20regard%20discipline%20as,sets%20me%20free%20to%20fly.

7. Jeanne Nakamura and Mihaly Csikszentmihalyi, "The Concept of Flow," *The Oxford Handbook of Positive Psychology*, 3rd ed., ed. C. R. Snyder, Shane J. Lopez, Lisa M. Edwards, and Susana C. Marquez (New York: Oxford University Press, 2009), 89–105.

8. Clay Risen, "Mihaly Csikszentmihalyi, the Father of 'Flow,' Dies at 87," *The New York Times*, October 27, 2021, https://www.nytimes.com/2021/10/27/science/mihaly-csikszentmihalyi-dead.html.

9. Daniel Goleman, "Concentration Is Linked to Euphoric States of Mind," *The New York Times*, March 4, 1986, https://www.nytimes.com/1986/03/04/science/concentration-is-likened-to-euphoric-states-of-mind.html?searchResultPosition=12.

10. "Football Association: British Sports Organization," Britannica, April 27, 2024, https://www.britannica.com/topic/Football-Association.

11. If you wish to review my research, please consult one of these publications:

    - Scott Juniper and Stephen Mellalieu, "The Impact of Role States on Team Effectiveness," *INSIGHT: The FA Coaches Association Journal* 4, no. 6 (2003): 59–61.

    - Stephen Mellalieu and Scott Juniper, "A Qualitative Investigation into Experiences of the Role Episode in Soccer," *The Sport Psychologist* 20, no. 4 (December 2006): 399–418, https://doi.org/10.1123/tsp.20.4.399.

    - Scott Juniper, "Clear Eyes, Full Hearts, Can't Lose," *Soccer Journal* 64 (September 2019): 52–53.

12. Rudyard Kipling, *The Jungle Book* (New York: Macmillan, 1894).

13. "Julie Andrews Quotes," Brainy Quotes, accessed June 2024, https://www.brainyquote.com/authors/julie-andrews-quotes#:~:text=Some%20people%20regard%20discipline%20as,sets%20me%20free%20to%20fly.

14. Rod Minchin, "Wales Football Legend Ivor Powell Dies Aged 96," *The Independent*, November 6, 2012, https://www.independent.co.uk/news/people/news/wales-football-legend-ivor-powell-dies-aged-96-8289825.html.

15. "Bison Bellows: The Winter Survivor," National Park Service, accessed June 2024, https://www.nps.gov/articles/bison-bellows-12-31-15.htm.

ACKNOWLEDGMENTS

The experiences and ideas from this book have emerged over a long period of time. I've been influenced by an endless list of people, through opportunities given to me by people who changed the course of my career.

Without the support of my wife, Jill, and our amazing kids, Glen and Faye, I wouldn't have had a chance. They deal with a dad who coaches sports and all of the chaos that comes with it. We love the opportunities it gives our family, but it takes a unique type of family support and understanding to make it all possible. Grandparents, Uncle, Auntie, Mum and Dad, Bro and Sis, Cuz and Cuz, you all shaped me growing up and helped build me into the coach I am today.

All of my friends and former teammates were part of my rich experience in sports, and I have nothing but happy memories of our games together and happier ones of the many celebrations after.

To every coach who mentored me through my journey when I was a player and to those coaches who offered guidance to me along my career path, you have all been a part of the lessons I have learned and shared in this book.

I want to thank the coaches I have played for over the years:

John Kirkwood, Jimmy, Graham Rushby, Alec Smith, Don Key, Vivien Juniper, Roy Massey, Alan Gilbert, Mr. Jones, Eric Johnstone, Geoff Harrop, Kevin Wesson, Phil Bloss, Chris Symes, Steve Pitt, Martin Toole, Steve Downman, Ian Alexander, Martin Durnell, Danny Iddles, Tony Passey, Ged Roddy, Paul Tisdale, Ivor Powell, and Steve Cochran.

Dr. Steve Mellalieu taught me the importance of precise language, and he guided me through the process of completing a master's thesis and publishing research in a peer-reviewed journal. Without Bret Simon trusting me with access to his program, half of that research wouldn't have happened the way that it did.

Without people opening doors for me at critical moments in my career, I would never have had the experiences that unfolded. Don Williams hired me when I was in long socks and fresh off the boat. David Deleon was the only one in the whole of Southern California who responded to my emails in the beginning, and he introduced me to Deb Schmidt who trusted me to coach her boys' teams. Tamiko Davila, Joey Hoffman, and Bart Hess gave me more opportunities to coach youth soccer. Steve Hoffman invited me to work with the Olympic Development Program. Kathy Hoffman always made me feel a part of the family. Mike Smith gave me my first shot with Region IV ODP, and "the dream team" made it a lot of fun. Tara Erickson, Nate Shotts, Platini Soaf, and Jerry Smith invited me back.

During my first Cal South ODP mission, it was Junior Gonzalez who persuaded Nat Gonzalez to add me to their staff at UC Riverside, and Junior handed me my first paid position in college sports a couple of years later. Thanks to all of these people who took a leap of faith with someone they hardly knew. I pay it forward whenever I can.

Some of these same folks spoke to April Heinrichs on my behalf, and her decision to make me her assistant coach was life-changing and pivotal in my career. Bob Chichester was the first athletic director to hire me as a head coach, and Mike Izzi and Paula Smith have signed the bottom of several contract extensions since then. Paul Hope has supervised our program for over a decade and has always been there with sage advice during the highs and the lows.

Jill Ellis and April invited me to work with US Soccer in a variety of roles, from scouting and development to assisting with youth national teams. As a lad from England, I felt honoured and humbled by these experiences. Working with the New Zealand national team for Head Coach Jitka Klimkova in a sports science role was another exceptionally humbling and rewarding experience for me. Thank you for trusting me to wear those crests. Those experiences have been so very special to me.

Tim Woodcock dreamed the big dream of pro soccer in Orange County, and he asked me to be their inaugural coach. Without Tim, Dave, Lana, and Adrienne, that team would never have been, and I am thankful to have been there at the beginning, working with amazing people and coaching some of the nation's top players.

PJ Woolridge and Danielle de Seriere have been coaching teammates with me at UCI for a decade, and Ludo Antunes added so much to our coaching family in the most recent seasons. The four of us have been through many adventures, and the ideas in this book have been heavily influenced by my journey with them. They have been rocks of granite for our program and our players. I am immensely grateful to everyone who opened doors and trusted me with special opportunities and experiences. Know that I've always given my fullest competitive efforts.

I've grown the program at UCI since 2007 with the support of some amazing people, including our coaches, strength coaches, athletic trainers, and operations staff. My UCI coaching teammates are as follows:

Katie Shields, Justin Neerhof, Kendall Fletcher, Karen Roos, Nikki Cheong, Mike Burns, Brad Ballard, Wendi Whitman, Peter Boyer, Geno Del Rosario, Heather Hathorn, Colette Swensen, Andy Winn, Bobby Harmston, Roxanna Gorji, Adam Doty, Richard Torvik, Bobby Harmston, Samira Kumar Varadharajan, Jackie Chan, Danielle de Seriere, PJ Woolridge, Nicole Lopez, Jill Radzinski, Janelly Farias, Bronson Sagon, Rachel Schmid, Jenny Chuang, Georgia Rieger, Ludo Antunes, Hannah Gates, Alyssa Gomez, Summer Williams, Rachelle Cyrus, Nico Ruiz, and Kailey Smith.

To all the players who have ever played for me, thank you for the blood, sweat, and tears we have shared pursuing our dreams through the beautiful game. Whether in camps, clinics, on ODP teams, semi-pro teams, national teams, or my college teams, I have loved every minute. I've had life experiences through soccer with you all that have helped me grow into the person, and the dad, that I am today.

For giving me the confidence, support, and encouragement to write this book, thanks to all my teammates at BrightRay Publishing. Without Warren and Ed, I wouldn't have got off the start line, and without Emily and Arjan, I wouldn't have found the finish line. Emily and Arjan, thanks for having fun throughout; I'll miss seeing you both on Friday mornings.

This is only half-time in my career, and documenting my ideas in this book has been challenging but hugely rewarding. At half-time, I tell my players that the job is only 30 percent done. This means I have many more adventures ahead with more amazing and inspiring people, and I can't wait. Thank you all in advance!

I'm only just getting started.

ABOUT THE AUTHOR

Coach Scott Juniper is building a legacy of transformation and has transformed the Anteater program into a formidable contender. In his role as head coach of UC Irvine women's soccer since January 2007, Scott holds the top winning percentage in Big West matches among active women's soccer coaches and ranks second-highest among both men's and women's coaches.

Over his 16-season tenure, Coach has guided the program to remarkable achievements including 12 winning seasons, 12 Big West Tournament appearances, ten 10-win seasons, and four Big West regular season championships. Under his leadership, the team has also secured three Big West Tournament titles with a historic three-peat in 2021, 2022, and 2023, and five NCAA Tournament appearances. The team has secured wins against top-tier programs like UCLA, USC, Cal Berkeley, BYU, Texas A&M, Auburn, Arizona, Arizona State, Oregon, Oregon State, and Wake Forest.

Through 170 career victories, Juniper's players have enjoyed significant individual success, including 96 All-Big West honorees, 28 All-West Region selections, 12 player-of-the-year awards, and two All-American honors. Anteater alumni have played professionally in 12 different countries. Three of his players have been inducted into the UCI Athletics Hall of Fame.

Juniper holds multiple coaching licences, including the US Soccer Federation "A" licence, UEFA "B" licence, US Soccer Federation National Youth licence, NSCAA Goalkeeper licence, and is a Certified Strength and Conditioning Specialist (CSCS). He taught a master's level course in advanced soccer theories at Concordia University for 10 years and has served as a coach educator for Cal South. He was also an age group head coach within the Olympic Development Program with Cal South and Region IV. Coach has also worked as a scout and assistant coach within the US Soccer Youth National Team program for a number of years and served in a sports science role for the New Zealand Women's National Team during the SheBelieves Cup in 2021.

Coach earned a bachelor's degree in psychology from the University of Bristol and a master's degree in sport and exercise science from the University of Bath, where he published his thesis on building high-performance teams in the peer-reviewed journal *The Sport Psychologist* (2006). His work was later featured in *INSIGHT: The FA Coaches Association Journal* (2003) and *Soccer Journal* (2019).

Scott, a native of Colchester, England, has settled in Newport Beach, California with his wife, Jill, and their two children, Glen and Faye.

Made in the USA
Middletown, DE
23 October 2024

62799503R00086